The Woman In The Room

HOW I REALIZED THE UNIQUE VALUE OF
WOMEN IN THE MALE-DOMINATED WORK-
PLACE

Dorothy Callihan

DEDICATION

To my daughters Stephanie and Allison

Special thanks to all the men and women I've worked with over the years who gave me the knowledge and experience for these books.

Content

Introduction

Women have passed knowledge down from generation to generation for centuries. Traditionally, that knowledge was limited to domestic life, child rearing and relationships. But now, with a growing number of women pursuing careers, it's time for women to share our knowledge and experience about being a woman in the workplace, especially the male-dominated workplace.

I've been immersed in male-dominated environments since the late 1970s when I went off to college to study engineering. I also enrolled in Air Force ROTC, which required membership in the Virginia Tech Corps of Cadets. It was during my freshman year that the Corps dissolved the all-female unit and integrated the women into the all-male units. So, between my classes and the Corps, I spent my college years surrounded predominantly by men, beginning a trend that would only intensify during my career.

After college, I was commissioned into the Air Force where I began my career in facilities management and construction. Back in the early 80s, it was rare for women to be in these industries, but that didn't deter me. I pursued roles and opportunities that were hard-core-male, usually making me the first woman my male colleagues had worked with as a peer. As my career progressed, I became their first female supervisor and manager. With few, if any female colleagues, when I attended a meeting in my workplaces, I was - The Woman In The Room.

Right from the beginning there was both curiosity and trepidation about a woman entering a men-only environment. I was often quietly warned that men were really good at business and then questioned as to whether or not I was sure I could measure up to their standard. This uneasiness never subsided and I was aware of the question that hung in the air whenever I started a new job: "Do you think she can handle it?"

My answer to the question came very early – on the afternoon of the fourth day of my career – when I stood in the middle of the office and said: "What the Hell?! I thought you guys were supposed to be good at this!"

For four days, I had witnessed chaos and crisis management. No one really seemed to be "in-charge" or even "taking-charge" as all the stereotypes suggested. My workplace didn't function according to anything I was told or any of the management theories I studied in in college. I didn't see a standard of performance that was at all intimidating – it was just the opposite. As I stood in the office, I shocked my colleagues when I said, "I am not working like this."

My declaration created a second parallel career track for me. While I learned the professional skills necessary to be a successful in facilities management and construction, I also intensely studied the male-dominated workplace. I was determined to fix how it did (or didn't) function. This second career track allowed me to hear, but ignore the continuum of career advice and narratives about the male-dominated workplace aimed at women like myself. By tuning out the outside noise, I tuned into what was going on around me.

Being the woman in the room, I had a unique perspective. I observed my male colleagues' natural and uninhibited behavior. I experienced the workplace men created – the pure male-dominated workplace, completely unaffected by women. For years I studied my male colleagues and questioned them about why they did what they did. I will admit that I also conducted lots of experiments and pushed many sensitive buttons just to see what reaction I would get.

At first, I couldn't articulate what was wrong with the way my workplaces functioned. It just seemed like there were things "missing" in everything they did, so I began using the term "Swiss cheese" to describe it. Since I already discredited the way they worked as substandard, I never felt I needed to copy men, fit in or become "one of the guys." This freedom allowed me to develop my own way of working in their Swiss cheese environment.

Working my way, I didn't compete with my colleagues as all the narratives suggested. Instead, I let them do their thing while I focused on identifying what they were missing and filling in their Swiss cheese holes. I noticed that once I filled the holes, our performance immediately soared. Consequently, I always out-performed all of my male colleagues - even those with 20-30 years more experience who were considered "the experts." After a few very high-profile successes, I knew I was onto something big.

I also knew that as a woman trying to transform how the male-dominated workplace functioned, I needed a mountain of credibility. So, I sought out and took on the biggest, most challenging and screwed up projects and operations I could find. I had to break through a lot of barriers, but I was determined to make sure no one could see me as the Token Woman or dismiss me with a pat on the head saying, "Well, Honey you did really well but, you only did the easy projects."

Over time and with a lot of trial and tribulation I became an expert at fixing my workplaces and I was eager to share my knowledge with men. However, I had a nagging thought. Nothing I was doing seemed all that revolutionary – actually it all seemed pretty obvious. So, I kept asking myself: "Why can't these guys, who have the same education and career experience as me, do what I'm doing?"

That turned out to be the billion dollar question.

There was only one difference between me and my colleagues - I was a woman.

Being a woman, I thought differently and had a different perspective than my male colleagues. By not trying to fit in, I gave myself permission to explore and develop my way of thinking and doing things. Eventually I realized that what was missing and what I filled in the Swiss cheese holes with were female characteristics. This is why my male colleagues couldn't replicate what I was doing and why I always enhanced what they were doing and got better results.

Today we often hear that companies with more women and female leadership perform better. However, we can only give a vague explanation of why that is because we are caught up in stereotypes and in erroneous narratives. These narratives originated before and during the early years of my career and weren't derived from women's actual experience. Instead they were written from our perspective outside the male-dominated workplace where we could only guess and assume we knew what was happening on the inside. Unfortunately these erroneous narratives endure and continue to block us from having the right information to advance our careers.

In order to advance women in the male-dominated workplace, we need to stop working off of 20th century assumptions. We need to challenge many of the ideas and concepts we learned as "truths" and hear more from women who can say, "Been there, done that and this is what worked." After we hear more from these still silent voices of experience, we can then rewrite our narratives so they are effective.

This book series begins that process of speaking from women's actual experience. In this first book I challenge conventional thought, correct the bad narratives and stop the misleading myths that have held women back. I define the major changes we need to make in our perceptions so we can discover and understand the unique value women bring to the workplace. I provide that critical explanation of exactly how and why women make companies perform better. Most importantly, I explain why empowering and advancing women in the workplace is critical to success in the 21st century.

Chapter 1
The Trail not Blazed

The women's liberation movement that began in the 1960s was the resurgence of the women's movement begun over 120 years earlier. Women needed to speak out again after years of silence because as we looked around at our post-World War II suburban existence, we asked "What am I doing with my life?"

Contrary to the images of a content 1950s suburban housewife, many women felt empty inside. We had limited outlets to express who we were and our personal identity was confined to wife and mother. We were financially dependent upon our husbands and forced to use his social status as our own. Following the convention of the time, we didn't even have our own name but were known as Mrs. John Smith or Mrs. Robert Jones. There was no question as to our dependency.

We yearned for the personal fulfillment we believed men had. Since their work gave them an identity, status, financial security and a purpose in the larger world, we went into the workforce too. However, we were no longer content to be secretaries, sales clerks, nurses and teachers. We wanted careers in professions that men dominated; careers that could take us to the top where we could find money and most importantly, power. We believed that once we had power we would have the ability to control our own lives.

My generation was the first large group of women to leave college with these huge aspirations. We were the second half of the Baby Boomer generation which has been more appropriately renamed Generation Jones. We were too young to participate in the protests and social conflict of the 60s but as young women we ready to reap its reward of women's equality.

Generation Jones was optimistic and idealistic. After growing up in an era of social unrest, we expected an era of peace to follow where all the new social ideas would take root, grow and blossom. In college, we embraced our equality as we aspired to redefine womanhood and women's roles in society. We were determined to blaze a new trail into the male-dominated workplace that future generations of women would follow to achieve full parity with men.

We expected our optimism to carry us through the challenges we knew were ahead of us. We accepted there were inherent differences between men and women because after all, there was no denying men were physically stronger. However in college we discovered women had a "smartness" men didn't have and we planned to leverage it to our advantage.

Today, Generation Jones women should be in the prime of their careers. Following our trail, millions of women should be CEOs, corporate board members, government leaders, senior managers and entrepreneurs of billion-dollar companies. But that hasn't happened.

As it turned out, career success was much harder to achieve than we expected. Our optimism turned into confusion, frustration, exhaustion and feelings of inadequacy. We were left Jonesing for the success and personal fulfillment we craved.

What went wrong?

We could blame the old standards of discrimination, biases and stereotypes, but that's way too simplistic of an answer. As Generation Jones women we were ready for all of that as well as a controlling and paternalistic, top-down hierarchal organization. We expected rude/crude comments, being "tested" and having to prove ourselves. Many of us already faced these issues in college, so we weren't naïve about the difficulties we would face in the workplace. We accepted that all of that stuff came with blazing a new trail for women.

The truth is that for many of us, the male-dominated workplace didn't live up to all of its bad hype if our male colleagues didn't think we had a "feminist chip on our shoulder." As we expected, our male peers were competitive, but– they were also friendly. In college we trained them to see us as equals and their wives reinforced the women's equality message at home. We also found there were older men from the Silent Generation who took a fatherly interest in us because their generation led the civil rights and women's liberation movements. They had a vested interest in our success and became willing mentors to many of us.

It was Baby Boomer men who surprised us. We believed they were driven by the social revolution of the 60s and would therefore be our greatest champions. But they weren't. Instead they were driven by their profound reverence for their fathers who fought in World War II. Their fathers were their heroes and they needed to prove themselves worthy of their father's hard work and sacrifices. In order to properly honor their fathers, Baby Boomer men needed workplace success and for younger men to admire and respect them just as they did their fathers.

Women who entered the male-dominated workplace to work on par with men threatened to disrupt this father-son dynamic. In response, Baby Boomer men held firm to the paternalistic workplace hierarchy and were often the most paternalistic men in the workplace. Their paternalistic behavior affected us but their real impact was on Gen X women who they shrewdly put in gender-neutral roles. These gender-neutral roles were historically held by men, but outside of the workplace promotion line. Feminists cheered as women "broke through barriers." Meanwhile Baby Boomer men kept quiet knowing the barriers women broke through led to a dead end and they had secured the line of respect and succession for Gen X men.

In spite of the acceptance we felt with many of our male colleagues, there was still something about the male-dominated workplace that made Generation Jones feel ostracized. Unfortunately, the reason we felt that way didn't make logical sense to us. Our male colleagues talked to us. They invited us to join them for lunch. We were friends outside of work. We were praised for turning in more complete and accurate work than our male peers. But even with this inclusiveness, we still felt like we didn't fit in and weren't accepted.

We suspected and feared our feelings were a female thing. Our feelings were fed on and intensified by the supposedly knowledgeable outside voices who told us that men set the highest business standard and we had to measure up. We felt pressure to emulate men because this was the only way we could prove that women were equal to men. But, as we noticed more differences between us and our male colleagues, we secretly feared we couldn't measure up and our presence would only prove that women didn't belong in certain roles.

The pressure to act like men included copying their loud and brash behavior because our narratives told us that it took a strong, confident personality to get to the top. We however wanted the workplace to be a meritocracy where we could leverage our smartness and be rewarded for producing better results. Consequently, women, who didn't want to adopt a personality they thought was obnoxious, gave up working the meritocracy and abandoned their careers. Our self-defeating narratives pushed many of my female peers out of the male-dominated workplace even though by all accounts they were successful, well liked, respected and could have gone far.

Our feelings of not fitting in were also fed by another secret we kept – we liked our femininity and being a woman. However, society didn't believe femininity belonged in the serious environment of the male-dominated workplace.

We were told not to allow our male colleagues to think of us as a woman. We were advised to look "professional," which meant dressing in shapeless black, navy and gray business suits so we didn't sexually arouse our male colleagues. We were told not to discuss any personal interests men associated with women, housewives or mothers. We were given ridiculous advice to watch sports and follow the scores so we had something to talk to our male colleagues about. This stereotyped advice assumed that men only talked about sports, but as we quickly learned, the stereotypes were wrong. We were shocked by how much our male colleagues opened up to us and confided in us about the most intimate details of their personal lives.

It seemed everyone else was immersed in the stereotypes and we stood as a bold, living contradiction to them. According to the stereotypes young women like us only went into the male-dominated workplace for one of two reasons: To look for a man or to become a man. We proudly declared that we weren't doing either and we worked because we wanted to. This spurred many workplace discussions where no topic about men, women and their respective roles was off limits. These discussions went far to broaden everyone's perspectives, correct assumptions and build rapport. They did more to achieve our equality than any other action until they were labeled politically incorrect and shut down.

Of course, no other issue brought women's femininity and roles to the forefront more so than motherhood. This was the hardest issue Generation Jones women faced because we openly challenged society's belief that motherhood and a career were incompatible.

In spite of women's liberation and birth control, society still assumed that once a woman married, she would soon become pregnant and stop working. We corrected this assumption. We stated we would become pregnant only when and if we were ready. We further stated that we didn't believe having children meant we had to stop working.

We expected our statement to shock our male colleagues but their reaction was sidelined by the firestorm we unleashed amongst women. Our statement divided women into two polarized camps who each pressured us to choose: Motherhood or Career.

We were completely caught off guard by this furor. To us, working mothers wasn't a new concept because our mothers did it. We weren't like the Baby Boomers who grew up in suburban Utopia. Our mothers were typically home while we were young, but by the time we were in middle or high school, they were forced into the workforce by a poor economy and sky-rocketing inflation. Our experience told us mothers had to work.

We learned however that society was still stuck in the 1950s where it was acceptable for mothers to work but only when their children were suitably "old enough." It was our idea that we could continue to work while our children were still babies and toddlers that unleashed the firestorm. Both sides dropped a mountain of guilt on us.

Stay-at-home-mothers told us that if we pursued a career and chose not to have children, then we weren't "real women." If we had children and continued to work, then we were unloving mothers who cast our children off to those horrible places called "daycare" while we selfishly pursued a career. At the time daycare centers were deemed a necessity to support low income and single mothers who had no choice but to work. The media regularly reported on the neglect, illness and deplorable conditions children suffered at daycare centers. Stay-at-home-mothers told us that only a woman who "had something wrong with her" would voluntarily send her children to daycare.

Feminists told us that if we gave up our careers to become stay-at-home-mothers, we were copping-out and admitting that women couldn't cut it in the workplace. Our failure would undo all the advances generations of women worked so hard to achieve and set women back for decades. On a personal level, we were warned that staying home would turn our brains to mush. We would lose all our professional knowledge and skills, thus making our careers irrecoverable. If and when we tried to return to the workforce, we would be relegated to low paying jobs.

Stay-at-home-mothers then countered by declaring that raising children and taking care of the home is "work" and harder than any office job. Their children were their careers and they proudly proclaimed motherhood as the noblest profession of all. To prove they had evolved from the 1950s housewife, they refused to identify through or subordinate themselves to their husbands. Mrs. Robert Smith became Matt's and Jenny's mother. Matt's and Jenny's success became their mother's success. Stay-at-home-mothers took motherhood to a whole new level of self-sacrifice and martyrdom that a working mother could never achieve.

Then, as if all this wasn't enough to contend with, reality piled on even more confusion.

For working mothers, daycare was often scarce and expensive! Daycare, professional clothes and car expenses ate up most of our income. Doing the math we questioned what we were gaining by abandoning all this precious time with our young children. Being a stay-at-home-mother seemed to make a lot of short-term sense.

But what did that mean long term? If we stayed home we couldn't afford all of the toys, activities, birthday parties, cars and college educations our children needed to meet Generation Jones expectations. We also thought about our financial future and golden retirement years. We knew we couldn't give our family the greater financial security we aspired to if we gave up our careers.

There were no good or right answers to end our confusion. So being true peace-loving, idealist, optimistic Jonesers, we decided we would appease everyone. We became Supermoms.

As Supermoms we proved women could have it all and do it all (except sleep). We set a new high standard and let everyone else try to measure up. If anyone wanted to play the martyrdom game, complain about how hard they had it or whine about how much they had to do, then they could just get in line behind us!

Naturally as time went on and we grew frustrated and exhausted. We began listening to that little voice inside ourselves that kept reminding us of the irony in our lives. As we tried to have it all and do it all, we felt like we were short changing every aspect of our lives. There was never enough time for work, our family, our marriage and "me-time" wasn't even a remote possibility. Ironically, our pursuit of personal fulfillment left us feeling inadequate and worthless.

As we examined our lives looking for help, we came up with one practical solution to our overloaded lives – we decided to impose gender equality on men. We demanded husbands help take care of children, do the dishes, help with the laundry and vacuum. At work we told men to type their own letters, book their own travel and make their own copies. Women finally found something we could all agree on.

Generation Jones witnessed women's lives go from being very boxed in with severe limitations to having no boundaries or guidelines at all. We didn't know what we were supposed to do or what was universally socially acceptable. We floundered and gave up trying to blaze a new trail for generations of women to follow as we each went our separate ways trying to figure out the best way to make our lives work for ourselves.

My path took me through all the iterations of a working woman. I began my career as a married Air Force officer. While on active duty I got my master's degree while simultaneously giving birth to two daughters with a husband who was deployed over 50% of the time. I was a Supermom on steroids and made it through due to the great support of my daycare provider Sandy. After I separated from the Air Force I fluctuated between Supermom and Stay-at-home-mom, learning how difficult it is to continue a professional career as an Air Force spouse.

Eventually we stopped moving and I restarted my career, but from a level lower than I had ever been before, earning only a third of what I made in the past. But the good news was that my brain didn't turn to mush. I still had more retained professional knowledge and skills than any of my peers. I began working the meritocracy and within three years I was back. I kept working the meritocracy and breaking through barriers until I finally reached the point where I needed career help to get myself to the next level.

By that time I had ventured deep into what one of my managers called "the Testosterone Zone." My peers and colleagues were the men who epitomized the stereotyped characteristics of success. To compete amongst these men, wasn't going to be easy so I researched the web hoping to find help. However, I was horrified by what I found. It was obvious the effort to advance women in the workplace hadn't evolved since 1970.

After reading through countless articles I began dividing them into groups. The first group was a myriad of feel-good and motivational articles. These articles and blogs played to the female stereotypes offering lots of empathy and letting me know other women were dealing with the same issues. They made me feel like my frustrations were heard and shared with the world. While these articles made me feel better they didn't offer any solutions. As an engineer and a business woman, I didn't want empathy. I wanted actionable solutions to help get me advance my career.

The second group had the opposite effect. These articles made me feel horrible. They said that the male-dominated workplace was inherently unfair to women. It doesn't matter what we do, how we act or what we achieve, the male-dominated workplace will always hold us back. They even said having more female managers won't help because women treat other women worse than men. These articles portrayed the average working woman as a hopeless, powerless victim.

I also read many studies and research papers that detailed all the ways in which women weren't reaching parity with men in the workplace. They were great at stating the problems, but just like the others they didn't offer any solutions. Therefore, they were worthless to me.

Frustrated I kept scouring the web. Finally I found the very small fourth group of articles that gave actionable solutions for women in the male-dominated workplace. I received one article that was circulating amongst women to rave reviews. However, I didn't like the article – there was something about it that really, really bugged me. Finally it hit me. I realized all of the solutions to advance women in the workplace could be summed up with the words I absolutely knew would not work: Act like a man.

Chapter 2
Am I a Man?

"I am more like a man than a woman."

I cringe every time I hear a woman say that. In recent years, I've heard countless women claim to be men, including women who to me look like they are very much a girlie-girl.

This statement has confused me ever since some young male colleagues several years ago informed me that I was really a man. After they said it, I did a quick body part inventory and concluded I was very much a woman. So, the only response I could muster up was a confused "What?"

Their response was even more confusing: "You're a man in a woman's body."

My gut reaction was to wonder what rock these guys just crawled out from under. If they were 60-year-old codgers then I would attribute their comment to the old stereotype that all career-minded women secretly want to be a man. But these were kids, Millennials fresh out of college. I concluded there were some new-fangled ideas about gender identity that was being taught on college campuses.

Since I like new ideas, I let their comment sink in – I am a man.

Did I have a gender identity crisis that I was completely unaware of?

Thinking about that for a few seconds, I again concluded I was a woman in every sense that I know. But wait – I am the only woman in my workplace in my job. That could only mean that "real women" don't do this job. Logically, that left only one possible explanation – there is something wrong with me. I am a mutant.

Using my sarcastic sense of humor, I then, in a very serious tone, informed my young colleagues, that I was tendering my resignation and taking my mutant self to Hollywood. I was sure I could get my own television reality show. I pictured myself in a Wonder Woman outfit holding an oversized nail gun, high into the air. After working with men for so long, I knew I had plenty of great story lines about the chaos and dysfunctions of the male-dominated workplace. My show was guaranteed to be a big hit!

Stunned, my young male colleagues tried digging themselves out of their hole. They explained they meant it as a compliment because I wasn't neurotically emotional. They said I was smart, rational, driven and better at my job than any of the guys. They even liked that I was a self-sufficient single working mother.

But then just as they were beginning to recover, they stepped onto a new land mine when they said, "You'll have a hard time finding a man."

Wow!

Does that mean men aren't attracted to smart, successful, self-sufficient women?

I asked them if I should interpret their comment as a formal notice of rejection from the male of the species and get "REJECT" tattooed across my forehead.

Even though I was slightly hurt by their comment, I knew my personal life didn't match their perceptions, but that was none of their business. So, I turned the tables and asked, "You're telling me that men only like emotional, submissive, needy women?" Then, looking directly at one young man I said, "I'll be sure to tell Lisa that." Then looking at another, "Should I tell Vicky too?"

That was the end of that discussion.

Even though these were young kids, their perceptions were right out of the 1960s. They made me wonder why after over 40 years, anyone would still perpetuate the idea that a woman who pursued a career and financial independence was more masculine than feminine. As a woman who spent her career in traditionally male roles, I was truly disappointed that society continued to perpetuate this myth.

Today we make distinctions between sexual identity and gender, which is only adding to the confusion for women. Because of my education and career choices I am considered a masculine heterosexual woman. I even listened to a panel of people on television discuss how women with career choices like mine should sexually identify as a woman, but gender identify as a man.

My only response to all this is: Sorry folks. I've worked with enough men to know the differences between me and them. I know I am 100% woman.

I am willing to go out on a limb and assume there are many women who like me who don't want their career choices, what they are good at or their desire for financial independence determine their gender or their femininity. Because I was so upset by this, I dug deeper to figure out what is at the heart of all this confusion.

Chapter 3
Separate Worlds

For centuries western culture used the Doctrine of Two Spheres to define men and women. It states that men and women, due to their biological makeup naturally inhabit two distinct and separate spheres.

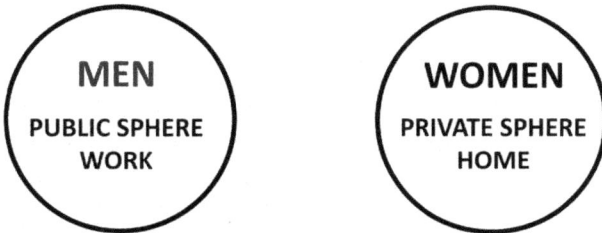

MEN
PUBLIC SPHERE
WORK

WOMEN
PRIVATE SPHERE
HOME

Men inhabit the public sphere of work, politics, law, business, commerce, academia and finance.

Women inhabit the private sphere of domesticity, child rearing and religious and charitable work.

To define "male" and "female" characteristics, we consider the role of each gender in their sphere. Men have all of the characteristics necessary to move society forward and create prosperity. Women have the characteristics necessary to raise children and create a happy home. The doctrine further states that since the spheres are distinct and separate, then men and women are distinct and separate. We do not share or even over-lap in our characteristics.

The Doctrine of Two Spheres affirms that in order to function and be successful in the public sphere one must have male characteristics. Therefore, a woman who pursues a career in the public sphere must leave her femininity and female characteristics behind in the private sphere. She will have the body of a woman, but she must think and act like a man.

After learning about the Doctrine of Two Spheres I wondered if the women's liberation or feminist movements ever challenged its validity as part of gender equality. To do so would say that male characteristics and female characteristics are of equal value in both spheres. However, I couldn't find any evidence of that nor do I ever remember hearing that. Instead, I remember equality being explained as: "Whatever men can do, women can do too." In other words, women can be the same as men.

Feminism fought for women's right to leave the private sphere and take up non-traditional roles in the public sphere. But in doing so it seems feminism accepted that men set the superior standard in the public sphere and fought for women to have the opportunity to measure up to their standard. Whether intended or not, feminism accepted that female characteristics didn't belong in the public sphere because they were inherently inferior and suitable only to the private sphere. It divided women between the superior career woman and the inferior stay-at-home-mother. That divide is still prevalent in the attitude of many women.

Today, we've modified the Doctrine of Two Spheres a bit by accepting that men and women share some characteristics. However, we still use the spheres as the basis to measure femininity and masculinity. For women whose lives span across both spheres, the doctrine creates confusion about our femininity. For example, how feminine do we consider a woman who works as an interior designer, but also competes in weight lifting? Or, how about a woman who works driving a cement truck, but bakes cakes to sell on weekends at the local market?

I became acutely aware of how confused we are soon after I began my website. One of the first articles I wrote questioned how we use workplace roles to label people as male and female. I was immediately lambasted by women who thought of themselves as men. It proved to me that many women still consider femininity inferior and therefore are afraid to be associated with it.

One of the women I had a lengthy exchange with insisted that she was a man and her husband a woman. I had read many of her posts which were very touchy-feeling so I didn't understand why she insisted she was a man.

She explained that both she and her husband were managers in technology companies and both were logical, rational and systematic. However, she made their gender assignments because her husband decorated their house. He chose the paint colors and painted the walls. He selected and arranged the furniture. He chose the accent pieces and decided where to hang the pictures on the wall. Because interior decorating is in the private sphere, she concluded that he is a "woman." Following this logic, since she isn't good at decorating and didn't help her husband at all, she is a "man." She went on to say that even with these gender assignments she was still "the mother" and her husband "the father" in raising their children.

She made my head spin because she was deeply entrenched in the Doctrine of Two Spheres, the stereotypes and the inferiority of private sphere. No matter what I said, I couldn't get her to take a step back to reexamine and broaden her perceptions. It became obvious she was afraid to be labeled "a woman" and be associated with decorating and domesticity because she was afraid of being seen as too feminine for her career field.

I am amazed that so many women still think like this since we proved back in the 20th century that using workplace roles to determine masculinity and femininity is nonsense. We proved women can be firefighters without turning into men. Men can be nurses without becoming feminized. Heck, even way back in 1970 no one thought my 5th grade elementary school teacher was anything but a manly man.

So, let's throw the Doctrine of Two Spheres into the trash can where it belongs. Let's forget all about men and women being suited for different roles. With the doctrine in the trash can we can start fresh. We can resume Generation Jones' aspiration to rewrite the definition of womanhood.

Chapter 4
New, True, Real Women

Whenever I read about the women of the early 20th century I wonder what happened to women. The women of the 1920s seemed so much more independent and liberated in comparison to the women of the 1950s and 60s. These women and those that came before them blazed an empowering trail for women that culminated in the right to vote and most women working prior to marriage. But then something happened. It seems we turned off the path that was advancing women, ventured off in a different direction and got lost. Trying to understand what happened, I read more about the women of the early 20th century. As I read a memory from when I was about 7 years old kept coming to mind.

I was shopping with my mother when she ran into two friends she knew from working as a nurse. They began a passionate conversation about the impact of women going into the workplace. They were concerned that no one would take over "women's job" in society. As I listened to their words my young imagination pictured crumbling and burnt-out buildings, hungry children, struggling mothers, crime and poverty. I understood that this community didn't come about simply because women weren't home to give their children milk and cookies after school. It existed because a dark, powerful force took over while women were too occupied at work to stop it.

I didn't understand this image until I learned about the women's movement that began around 1820. This movement, called True Womanhood[1], made women responsible for maintaining a moral and civilized society. This was the "women's job" my mother and her friends were talking about. In the 1960's people feared that if women "became masculinized" and went into the workforce, we would also abandon our feminine role as protectors of society. The void we left would be filled by controlling, patriarchal, male-dominated entities that would further subjugate women as it released men from their family responsibilities. Male energy would take over all aspects of society, destroying the private sphere and society.

From our perspective today, this seems a bit dramatic until we consider the stereotyped male characteristics of aggression, competitiveness, control and power. We have to ask ourselves if empowering more male energy and allowing it to dominate both the private and public spheres is good for society. This was the dilemma women faced as the women's liberation movement gave women permission to copy and act like men.

The women's liberation movement shunned True Womanhood and its ideals. It blamed True Womanhood for endorsing a patriarchal society and the subjugation of women. Growing up in this era, I shared this attitude as I rejected what I believed True Womanhood stood for - submission and obedience to men, shame for losing your virginity prior to marriage and finding personal fulfillment in vacuuming and cleaning the bathroom. But, as I read more, I found elements of True Womanhood I really liked. There seemed to be some long forgotten truths about womanhood buried in the ideals.

At first, I thought I should be ashamed of myself. But as I kept reading, I stopped looking at True Womanhood from a 21st century

---

[1] Most information and writing about True Womanhood is based the work of Welter, Barbara, "The Cult of True Womanhood: 1820-1860." American Studies University of Virginia, 1966, http://xroads.virginia.edu/~DRBR2/welter.pdf

perspective and put it in the context of the 19th century when women had no rights and were completely dependent on men. That's when it made sense. I stopped seeing these historical women as weak, subservient, emotional or silly. They were smart and strong. They manipulated their vulnerability into power and blazed the trail that generations of women and feminists followed. True Womanhood began the 19th century progression of women to Real Womanhood, Public Womanhood and eventually to the very progressive New Womanhood of the 1920s. In the 100 years from 1820 to 1920, women went from having no voice, to having the voice that shaped society and the right to vote. They created the greatest era of women's empowerment in history.

Unfortunately this is the path we turned off of and lost. If we want to advance women then we need to find it again and learn its lessons.

The 19th Century Perspective

To understand why women rose up and asserted their voices in the early 19th century, we have to understand the Industrial Revolution and dramatic cultural changes it created.

Before the Industrial Revolution, most men and women worked side by side making their livelihood in or around the home. The Industrial Revolution disrupted and changed that. Families moved to the cities where men for the first time left the home to go to work. Husbands and wives now spent their days in two distinctly different environments imposing the Doctrine of Two Spheres on a much larger section of society.

For women this change was easier to cope with – they could still ground themselves in the familiarity of their home, domestic tasks and children. Living in close quarters with other families meant there were other women around they could lean on. But for men, the change was dramatic. The Industrial Revolution created a new order and changed how men perceived their place and value in society.

Education emerged as a discriminator, changing our definition of the ideal and powerful man. It distinguished between the educated men who worked with their heads to plan and manage the work from the men who were forced to work with their hands because they were perceived as too stupid to be educated. Consequently, the typical factory worker was demeaned and seen as nothing more than expendable brawn to power the industrial machine. With physical strength no longer a factor, the most important male characteristic to determine a man's superiority became an intelligent and forceful personality capable of intimidating others. This new ideal man, using callous and calculating thought, created a vicious and ruthless public sphere. Society and its churches recognized the damage and havoc these men could inflict on the rest of society if they weren't controlled. The ideals of True Womanhood emerged.

True Womanhood and its four virtues of Piety, Purity, Submissiveness and Domesticity called upon women to balance the darkness of the public sphere. Women were to guard against men's behavior invading the private sphere and taking further advantage of the already precarious situation of women and their children. It declared the private sphere and the home in particular as a woman's domain. It expected women to make the home a sanctuary that nurtured men's gentler, moral and aesthetic traits in order to balance the ugly characteristics they cultivated in the public sphere. The home is where a woman asserted her power and influence over her husband.

Although True Womanhood defined the ideal for all women, the vast majority of women were too busy just trying to get by to meet its stringent standards. Only upper class women with domestic help had the capacity to aspire to be True Women. These women used the ideals to showcase their husband's wealth and success which may explain its lasting influence amongst the rest of society for social climbing.

Piety – The Ultimate Power Grab

True Womanhood's first virtue of Piety declared that Religion, by divine right, belonged to women. Our inherent nature made it easier for women to be closer to God and project his will into society. Women were to be a bright light that shined out into the world, attracting and drawing men away from the darkness of the public sphere. Piety is what gave women moral superiority over men.

True Womanhood, believed women's religious role was so critical that women shouldn't engage in any pursuit that took their focus away from God or the private sphere. While women could attend female colleges, studies were limited to subjects consistent with religion and the private sphere. If women needed activities to occupy their time, then they were to delve into religious or charitable work. Piety protected women from being tainted by the darkness of the public sphere by confining them to the private sphere. True Womanhood knew that if women acted like men, they would lose their moral superiority and all the power that came with it.

As I read about Piety a couple things immediately struck me. First, I liked the idea that women shine a bright light out into the world. This makes standing up for what is moral, right and good an inherent part of womanhood. Piety gave women a larger purpose in the world other than just wife and mother – women were the guardians of the greater common good.

Secondly, I was surprised that religion belongs to women. I thought our paternalistic society kept religion within the male domain and used religion to subjugate all women below all men because it was Eve who was tempted by the serpent and convinced Adam to eat the forbidden fruit. Eve was to blame for mankind getting kicked out of the Garden of Eden and it's women's fault that the world is a dark place.

Piety wiped all of that blame and guilt away. It reversed society's belief as to who was the bearer of darkness and who was the bearer of light. Piety inferred men's weaknesses, inferiority and flaws as it pulled off one of the greatest female manipulations of all time. In an era when women had no legal power and could only assert themselves by aligning with or marrying a powerful man, these clever women aligned themselves with the most powerful "man" of all – God. To defy women was now to defy God himself.

Piety covertly challenged the patriarchy which declared that men had the right to decide what is in the best interests of their female family members and children. Women's moral authority officially gave women the power to raise their hand and object to men's decisions. And churches backed them up.

Therefore, we should see Piety as an enormous, shrewd and covert power grab. The severe restrictions Piety placed on women was to prevent them from eroding this fragile power base. Keeping it intact enabled them to build upon it and increase their influence in society.

Throughout the 19th and early 20th centuries, women, with the backing of churches, increasingly exploited their moral authority to extend their reach deep into the public sphere. They used their church community to gather and unite women who together argued for social changes that benefited women, children, families, the sick and the poor working class. They led the abolition and temperance movements. Piety gave women the right and fortitude to defy the will and power of men in order to stand up for what was right, moral and in the best interest of the greater common good. Eventually women used their influence to obtain legal power through the right to vote and hold political office.

Purity - The Power of "No"

Piety presumed women were non-sexual, but still vulnerable to seduction by men just as Eve was seduced by the serpent. This brought about the second virtue of Purity which declared a woman's virginity as her greatest treasure - only to be given away on her wedding night. Fear and shame were used to scare women into upholding this virtue with stories how of "fallen women" were shunned, could go mad, or in the very least never marry because no good and decent man would marry a non-virgin.

Women were told to expect men to make advances and for men to even be aggressive in their advances. A True Woman however remained strong and withstood all advances. By remaining pure, a woman proved her superiority and power over men. She also helped men raise their own virtue – a True Woman could elevate a man and save him from himself.

Today we reject True Womanhood's Purity for many reasons, particularly the shame it levied on women. However, we must remember that this virtue existed in the days before birth control, safe abortion, welfare, daycare and employment opportunities for mothers. For 19th century women the consequences of being pregnant and abandoned by the father were dire. Unwed mothers who didn't have their family's support were often forced into prostitution where disease and abuse quickly took their toll. Their orphaned children were often left to fend for themselves on the streets. True Womanhood believed the best way to protect children and give them financial security was to ensure they were born to married parents.

Purity empowered women to stand up for and protect themselves and their future children. True Womanhood believed that if women told men "No" to unacceptable behaviors and held to that conviction, then men, wanting to please women, would respond positively. Likewise, if women allowed men to take advantage of them, men would. Therefore, it was up to women to use their moral authority and the power of "No" to draw and enforce the lines of acceptable male conduct.

Today women still use the power of "No" to set lines of acceptable behavior with men. Many men still believe in women's moral authority and have a desire to look good in the eyes of women. This is applies to the workplace as well and explains a situation I frequently experienced with my male colleagues.

When I expressed simple disappointment in a man's performance, I often got a sulking or pouting response. I would think, "What did I do that hurt his feelings so much?" I didn't act like one of male colleagues who would have yelled or cussed him out. I'd seen men treat each other like that many times and they were fine. Why did I get a different response for being nicer?

The answer was simply that I am a woman expressing disappointment in a man's conduct and that had a profound affect. I was using the power of "No" without realizing it. Later in my career, when I was a manager, I learned how to effectively leverage the power of "No" to assert myself and my authority.

Submissiveness – To God, Not Men

True Womanhood's third virtue of Submissiveness suggests an endorsement of a patriarchal society where men oppress women and women docilely comply. I will admit that I struggled to understand this virtue because it seems to contradict the empowering aspects of Piety and Purity. I just couldn't imagine that women, who already had no rights or power, purposely designed and endorsed a culture that intensified their subjugation and vulnerability to men. That's when it dawned on me that I had to stop seeing True Womanhood through a 21st century perspective. Submissiveness as a virtue only makes sense when we put in the context of the era.

In the 19th century the fledgling United States experienced the Industrial Revolution and westward expansion. It needed brazen, strong and confident men to drive the country forward and make it a player on the world stage. These men needed to believe they could overcome any challenge placed before them. If they gave up or quit, it was analogous to submitting to a more powerful force and allowing it to determine your fate. For men trying to build a country, submissiveness was unacceptable as a male characteristic.

Therefore, in keeping with the Doctrine of Two Spheres, submissiveness had to be a female characteristic.

Piety also dictated submissiveness as a female characteristic because it required women to submit to the will of God. Submissiveness forced women to subordinate their personal ego in order to elevate their support of the greater common good. Ironically, this higher pursuit gave women a reason to not blindly submit or accept the will of their husbands.

Our modern criticism of Submissiveness comes from how True Womanhood told women to be timid, dependent, childlike and grateful for a husband who was their heroic protector from the outside world. But this says less about who women were supposed to be and more about who women needed men to be.

Without their own rights and legal standing, women assumed their husband's power and influence as their own. Therefore, women desired a husband who was wealthy, mentally strong, intimidating and unquestionably superior. The Doctrine of Two Spheres encouraged women to exaggerate their own weaknesses so they could then exaggerate their husband's strength and power. This way, when it suited her, a woman could lift the veil of Submissiveness to wield her husband's influence and status in accomplishing her social objectives.

We shouldn't attach our definition of submissiveness and its implication of inferiority to the era. Submissiveness didn't imply that all women were inferior to all men – upper class women certainly didn't see themselves as inferior to the uneducated men who worked on the factory floor. In reality many women weren't as submissive to their husbands as the standard implies which explains a phrase I often heard growing up "Submissive – That's what we let men think." The reality was that the captains of industry like today's plutocrats didn't marry childish, insipid women. They married their equal – their wives, like them were a force to be reckoned with.

Ironically, we now think of Submissiveness as keeping women dependent on men and making them incapable of changing their fate. In reality it had the opposite effect. Submissiveness empowered women to act on behalf of God's will and assert their influence over men and society. This changed society and their fate.

Domesticity – The Path to Financial Independence

The last virtue, Domesticity confirmed the home as a woman's domain; it was their power base where they used the power of "No" to set the standards of conduct. In the home, women exercised their influence over their husbands to bring them back to God, family, fatherhood, church and community. Just as women do today with giving their husband a man cave, True Womanhood encouraged women to make the home a sanctuary and a loving, cheerful place in order to keep their husband and his friends at home and out of taverns, gambling parlors and brothels. As with all the virtues, women had an underlying objective to protect themselves and their children from their vulnerabilities. By keeping their husbands at home, women hoped to prevent their husbands from squandering money and threatening the family's financial security.

True Womanhood expected women to revel in any task associated with the home as an expression of their femininity. Domestic tasks such as needlepoint, music, flower arranging, caring for children, cooking and housekeeping were considered uplifting tasks. In reality, housekeeping and cooking were arduous chores, but the upper-class women who aspired to True Womanhood could delegate those tasks to their domestic help without compromising their delicate feminine qualities.

Even though the ideals of True Womanhood weren't achievable for most women, Domesticity emerged as the virtue that unified all women in a common bond of womanhood and femininity. Even in the most austere conditions women used Domesticity to find a way to connect with their femininity. A woman traveling to the west in a covered wagon, or cooking over an open fire in a small cabin or doing laundry in a miner's camp could pick wildflowers for display or put them in her hair. She could add a bit of embroidery to the most basic piece of clothing or linen to provide that feminine touch.

Domesticity had a practical benefit too - it blazed the trail that led women to greater employment opportunities and financial independence.

Any situation where there were a lot of men and very few women was an economic opportunity for women who offered domestic services. During the gold rushes and westward expansion women could make a living cooking, baking, sewing, doing laundry or running a boarding house. They often fared better financially than their male counterparts.

Domestic skills eventually transitioned women into new professions. Women who cared for the sick in the home were called upon during the Civil War to care for injured soldiers. As a result of war, nursing became a female profession. Likewise, women's child rearing experience was a good fit for teaching and women filled many vacant teaching positions as men also transitioned to new professions.

The Civil War and westward expansion resulted in fewer men residing in the most populous states. This and an expanding economy left many jobs vacant and women with fewer marriage prospects. Women who needed to support themselves were recruited to fill a variety of jobs. One of the first ways women demonstrated a unique skill in the male-dominated workplace was as typists. Their small nimble fingers adept at needlepoint were well suited for the typewriter keyboard.

By the end of the 19th century many women spent a few years in the workforce prior to marrying. With paying jobs as an option, women were no longer financially dependent on men and could be choosier about who they married. The average age women married rose slightly to 22 which was older than in the 1950s and 60s when women's average marrying age reached its lowest point of about 20 years old.[2] This makes us wonder what happened in the mid-20th

---

[2] "Median Age at First Marriage, 1890-2010." Infoplease.
https://www.infoplease.com/us/marital-status/median-age-first-marriage-1890-2010

century that caused women to make a U-turn and lose much of the financial independence and empowerment we already achieved.

Learning From Our Past

In the history of women, True Womanhood is important because it reminds us of women's inherent power to influence men for the better. To me it raised a very important question: If women's influence can elevate men's behavior in the private sphere, then why can't we assert that same influence in the public sphere to better men, our workplace and society as a whole?

True Womanhood made standing up for the greater common good the unifying core value of womanhood and femininity. Therefore, when women go into the male-dominated workplace today, we should do so with the added purpose of standing up for what is right and good and fair. We should be the bright light that brings the public sphere out of darkness.

For women to be effective bearers of light, then women must be actively involved in all workplace roles across all industries. We must be in the all of the conference rooms and in all of the closed doors private meetings where men talk themselves into taking immoral, unethical or even illegal action. Once in there, we need to assert our influence and know how to effectively leverage our power of "No" to stop the bad decisions that lead to destructive action.

Our support for the greater common good also extends to influencing how our workplace functions and performs. We have a duty to ensure the workplace is efficient, productive, innovative, gratifying to its employees, attentive to its customers and consistently profitable. We want our workplace to thrive and grow so it can continue to provide opportunity and financial security for all of its employees and their families.

Chapter 5
I Want a Hero

I consider myself fortunate that the stereotypes weren't a factor in my upbringing. By the standards of the 1950s, my parents were very different - they married and began a family in their late 30s. My mother, prior to marrying, supported herself as a nurse and even purchased her own home. No one ever called her weak, timid or submissive and any man who thought he could patronize the petite blond lady, quickly learned differently. In high school when I had to write a report either supporting or opposing the women's liberation movement, I wrote that it wasn't an issue because my mother was already liberated. And following her example, I was too.

My father was an electronics engineer who expected his daughters to go to college just as his sister, mother and grandmother had done. He saw how the Great Depression and World War II impacted women and their children, so he encouraged me to get a degree in engineering. He always told me that you never know what will happen in life so I should learn a profession that allowed me to support myself and my children on my own. I always considered this very wise advice for all women.

So, while I was aware of the stereotypes, they never had any meaning to me. I never thought they accurately described women or were something for women to aspire to. To me, they represented fairytale and romance novel characters – strong valiant men and sweet women who needed a male hero to rescue and take care of them. They didn't represent the real life of my family or any family I knew.

Female		Male	
Submissive	Timid	Dominant	Brave
Dependent	Content	Independent	Ambitious
Unintelligent	Passive	Intelligent	Active
Emotional	Cooperative	Rational	Competitive
Receptive	Sensitive	Assertive	Insensitive
Intuitive	Insecure	Analytical	Confident
Weak	Appreciative	Strong	Judgmental

Given the accomplishments of women through the mid-20th century, the stereotypes should have died out long ago. World War II proved women were capable of stepping up and filling vacant male jobs in every capacity. My mother was representative of the women of the Greatest Generation – they were strong, feisty women, who took pride in doing their part. They were role models whose actions should have propelled women forward by leaps and bounds but we went backwards instead.

What happened?

The men who fought in World War II were true heroes. They were moral, honorable men who were victorious in their mission to defeat truly evil men. They weren't the kind of men women needed to protect society from - they were just the opposite. They were our ideal men, our real life knights in shining armor who valiantly risked their lives to defend us. They made the United States a super-power and put us on the right side of the Cold War. They earned the right to be looked up to and revered.

As our heroes took back their traditional roles we also let them claim moral superiority as theirs. They restored the old paternalistic order. The empowerment women got from True Womanhood's

Piety faded away. Our submissiveness to God transformed into submission to the men we put up on a pedestal. Many women lost their greater sense of purpose as society and media images shrank our influential private sphere to an isolated kitchen in a suburban house. Without a larger moral purpose in society, the stereotypes became many women's identity.

Whether we did it intentionally or not, we set aside our own inherent power to be wooed by the romance of male heroes. Our idealization of men affirmed the superiority of male characteristics. However our worst mistake was that we gave ourselves permission to sit back and let men take care of us. We diminished ourselves to elevate men and their masculinity.

Rosie the Riveter needed her husband to talk to the plumber, the electrician and the car mechanic because she just couldn't understand what they were talking about. Women who managed family and business finances during the war became financially vulnerable and ignorant of the family finances with the excuse, "My husband takes care of that because I'm not good at math." Women didn't experience the workforce because they dropped out of college to get married and become a housewife. Our desire to marry our own hero encouraged women to be the childlike creatures we believed True Womanhood idealized.

The reality was that many women liked and protected the paternalistic structure. It was a safety net that negated our need to take risks, challenge ourselves or advance ourselves in society because it made men responsible and duty bound for supporting the family. Simply put, the patriarchy gave women permission to play it safe. We could be fulltime housewives or have "secondary careers" while we pushed our husbands to success.

Women also secretly liked marriage and the patriarchy because it gave us a shortcut to power. If we married high status or wealthy men, we didn't have to fight our way up from the bottom – we could just piggyback off our husband's success, influence and connections. In comparison to men, few women have worked their way up from nothing to the plutocracy based solely on the merit of their actions. Historically, most women in high government or corporate power positions had a male family member or a husband pave the way by obtaining a high power position first. So, while we may not always like the patriarchy, we aren't in a rush to dismantle it either because we have a vested interest in the patriarchy working in our father's or husband's favor. And whatever works in their favor, works in our favor too.

Realistically, we also need to retain the patriarchy's sense of responsibility and duty to the family because there is no denying that having children increases women's financial vulnerability. If we choose to stop working or pull back on our careers to focus on our children then we must rely on our husbands as the primary bread winner. However, this doesn't give us permission to bury our heads in the sand and be naïve.

Our lives aren't static. As my father said, you never know what will happen - there is divorce, illness, injury, death, economic down turns, debt and job loss. Stay-at-home-mothers find themselves forced back in the workplace. Women who put their careers secondary to their husband's become the primary or the only source of income. To go through life relying on men to provide our financial security is a risky gamble in which we and our children are the losers.

Many women fought for women's rights so we were no longer vulnerable and dependent on men. But in order to exercise our full rights and accept our responsibility for our welfare, we have to let go of our idealism for men. We have to take them off the pedestal we keep them on. We can no longer believe they set a higher standard, have power women can't access or have some kind of magical male privilege that protects them from fate. I know, after working with thousands of men, there is nothing extraordinary about men – they are all just regular and ordinary guys.

As women, we must believe in our own inherent power and believe that it can be different from men's but still be fully equal to men's. So, let's throw the stereotypes and idealist male heroism into the trash can with the Doctrine of Two Spheres. Once we do that, we can embrace who we inherently are and get back on the path so many women worked hard to blaze for us. As we move forward on this path, we will discover and define how men and women should interact in the 21st century as full equals.

Chapter 6
Women Hold Up Half of the Sky

There is an ancient Chinese proverb that says, "Women hold up half the sky." This proverb presents us with a very different image of women by stating that we are an essential half of the whole. This makes women full equals to men but with a different and unique value.

Thinking of women as half of the whole is a radical departure from what we are taught. It means that no matter how big and strong or heroic men are, they can't hold up the entire sky. It means we no longer have to fight men to hold up their piece of their sky or demand they give us a piece of their sky because we have our own. Our half of the sky gives us power and purpose equal to men's. Most importantly, it means we haven't been working and living in wholeness like we thought.

As we continue to look at Eastern philosophy we see the image of women holding up half the sky represented in the Yin and Yang concept we are familiar with. It is unlike the Doctrine of Two Spheres which divides male and female into two static and separate spheres where they can't influence each other and interact. Instead, Yin and Yang are connected opposites. They continually interact and influence each other, creating a dynamic environment. Neither is superior or inferior, each controls the other and both need the other to create a harmonious whole.

True Womanhood shrewdly introduced this concept to western culture when it described women's role in the private sphere. In the home, women asserted their influence to control their husband's darker side and draw out his positive qualities. This male-female interaction aspired to make the home harmonious and whole. This same concept now needs to be applied to the workplace, but we have to be careful. Our culture can easily trick into seeing Yin and Yang in terms of the old stereotypes.

When we see lists of Yin and Yang gender characteristics, Yin and female energy are typically assigned passive and less energetic characteristics, while Yang and male energy are assigned active and energetic characteristics. This automatically reminds us of the stereotypes. Yang characteristics such as controlling, logical, rational and aggressive lead us to conclude Yang is dominant and superior. However, that kind of thinking overlooks the entire Yin and Yang concept of complementary and interdependent characteristics to create harmony, balance and wholeness.

Yin	Yang
Inward	Outward
Yielding	Controlling
Being	Doing
Creative	Analytical
Intuitive	Rational
Emotional	Logical

The stereotypes and our culture's favoritism for Yang and male energy have always misled us into believing the male-dominated workplace doesn't need Yin. However, this belief has resulted in our workplaces being out of balance and inefficient. Our workplaces have results and performance that fall short of expectations. They have problems that are never completely solved. The supposed solutions create new problems and unintended consequences which create frustration, chaos and crisis management. We see this happening everywhere and it's because Yang is working by itself.

Today's problems come from yesterday's "solutions."
- Peter Senge[3]

The problems created by Yang working alone are what I saw the first week of my career. I felt there were things "missing" in my workplace because I felt its incompleteness. Being incomplete and out of balance, it couldn't function properly. This situation was repeated in every one of my male-dominated workplaces and to correct it I had to challenge a lot of conventional thinking.

Like my male colleagues, my education as an engineer and my career choices taught me to use Yang thinking to solve problems and get things done. I was taught to be analytical, rational, systematic, logical and objective. While I could do this, there was something about it that felt off. I didn't like distancing myself from a problem or situation in order to be objective. I never felt objectivity provided me with the best solution.

My male colleagues frequently used expressions like "Don't get down in the weeds" and "You can't see the forest for the trees" as their rational for keeping their distance. As I discovered, these are Yang expressions because they tell us that to deal with a problem (the forest), you must remove and distance yourself from the details (the trees). It is the opposite of the Yin approach which believes that

---

[3] Senge, Peter *The Fifth Discipline The Art & Practice of The Learning Organization*, New York: Doubleday, 1990, pg. 57

if there is a problem then we have to be in the forest and amongst the trees to solve it. That is the only way we can really understand what is going on.

Throughout my career I've been counseled many times for not acting like a manager and getting "too far down in the weeds." However, by combining what I was taught with what I felt was right I achieved balance and solved problems holistically. I got down in the weeds to interact with my team and understand the situation from their perspectives. No one was too far beneath me to talk to. Then, I distanced myself so I could objectively think about the problem and come up with ideas. I then went back to my team and we bounced ideas off each other. By going back and forth like this, my team and I understood the problem completely and developed complete solutions. This of course took time which was contrary to the Yang need for an immediate answer. However, I ignored the pressure to shoot from the hip and let my results speak for themselves. Later in my career, I turned the tables and chastised many fellow male managers for keeping too much distance, for not getting down in the weeds and allowing problems to perpetuate.

I always knew the incompleteness I experienced in all of my workplaces came from how my male colleagues didn't work together right. Several people were assigned to a project and each of us was given our task to do in support of the larger project. We each then worked on our project independently. As the woman in the room I wanted to talk to my male colleagues about what I was doing and what they were working on but I noticed none of the men were talking to each other about their tasks. And our manager didn't go around and follow up with us either. He simply held status report meetings where everyone affirmed they would get their task done on time.

As an engineer, I understood the Yang logic and rational of why my male colleagues worked and managed as they did. The project was too large and complex for any one person to complete so it was broken down into different tasks and assigned to us based upon our our knowledge and experience.

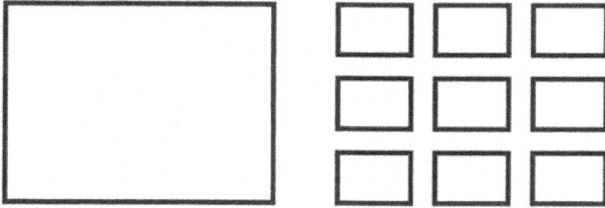

By fragmenting the project into smaller pieces it was easier for our manager to objectively sort, arrange, list and track the pieces on his board. He could think about and manage one task at a time. Meanwhile, my male colleagues who didn't talk to each other about their tasks, completed their tasks independently according to their expertise. It was assumed that using their expertise they would complete their tasks the optimum way. But, on the deadline day, when all the pieces/tasks were brought back together they didn't fit together properly. This resulted in panic, chaos, crisis management and inefficiency as a slew of new last minute problems had to be addressed.

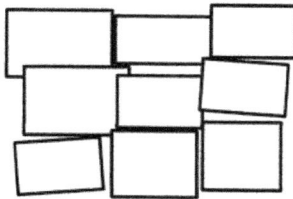

The male-dominated workplace doesn't understand the real root cause of its performance issues and why they perpetuate. For decades, I watched it try to fix its issues through technology and a series of new management initiatives. These measures ultimately fell short of expectations or faded away into oblivion because they didn't address the fundamental underlying problem – too much reliance on Yang energy.

In order to correct performance issues, the male-dominated workplace must work in wholeness which means all the pieces must work in unison and in harmony. The only way to do that is by keeping them connected to each other at all times.

So, how do we keep them connected?

We use the Yin energy we dismissed a long time ago as inconsequential.

Creating Wholeness

To create wholeness Yin and Yang must continuously interact. This means all workplaces in all industries need our female energy, thinking and ways of doing things across all roles. It also means women have to stop copying men. We no longer try to lift their half of the sky, fight them for a piece of their sky or demand that they give us a piece of their sky. Our focus has to be on lifting up our half of the sky.

You probably heard the narrative that when men and women are given an assignment they respond differently. Men take their piece/task and immediately rush into action. Women however, start talking and forming relationships. Our culture admires men's immediate rush to action and dismisses our relationship building as touchy-feely stuff and female timidity. However, what we are really doing is empowering the Yin. We talk to each other so we can learn and understand the relationship between all the pieces/tasks so we know how they are connected. We want to know how the individual pieces/tasks interact, influence and impact each other. We claim our way is better while men claim their way is. In actuality, neither men nor women have the best approach. The best approach is found by combining the two. Think of it this way:

- Men and Yang break apart or fragment the big picture so they can apply their expertise to individual pieces.
- Women and Yin understand the relationships so we can connect the pieces.

- When we connect men's individual pieces using women's relationships we create the whole.

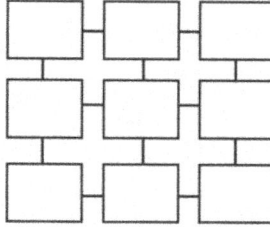

Because wholeness requires understanding the relationship amongst all the pieces/tasks, relationships are no longer just touchy-feely stuff. They are the essential other half. Wholeness states that men's action and women's relationships are of equal value and therefore men and women are of equal value.

When we work in wholeness we put the whole into action, not just the individual pieces. This is what all of us we have been asking our workplaces to do without even knowing it.

Have you ever had the experience where you got information off your computer or had a task pass onto you from another colleague and it wasn't what you needed, it was incomplete or in the wrong format? You got upset with your colleague because you believe he didn't know how to do his job. However, the problem isn't that your colleague is incompetent – it's that no one has addressed the relationship between your two tasks so work can flow smoothly and efficiently from him to you.

When we empower the Yin, we correct that problem. We address how tasks and people have to interact and work together to achieve a goal, provide a service, produce a product or solve a problem. This is working in wholeness.

The biggest obstacle our workplaces have to overcome to work in wholeness is overcoming the belief that Yang energy is all powerful. We have this crazy idea deeply embedded in our culture that we can make up for the absence of Yin if we just apply more and more Yang. We find this thinking in all of our workplaces, leadership courses and management books. We don't understand that it is the biggest mistake we make.

It took me many years to read through the book *The Fifth Discipline, The Art and Practice of the Learning Organization* by Peter Senge because I kept getting frustrated. As I read the book I kept finding myself yelling at it, "Just tell companies to hire more women! They will explain it" and putting it down. Finally I realized that Peter Senge never considers that many of the concepts he discusses come from the Yin. He spends 400 pages trying to explain Yin through Yang thinking.

Likewise, in his famous book *Good to Great,* Jim Collins talks about creating the flywheel effect[4] which countless companies tried to replicate. He describes it as the slow but steady build-up of achievements that create the momentum for even more achievement. According to Jim Collins the flywheel gets moving "by a cumulative process - step-by-step, action-by-action, decision-by-decision, turn-by-turn of the flywheel - that adds up to sustained and spectacular results."[5]

But, this is a description of fragmented Yang action. It is trying to create the dynamic interaction of Yin and Yang using only Yang and it doesn't work.

Look at the symbol for Yang all by itself. If we try to make it rotate, it will start to rise but then it will roll back down. It can't roll

---

[4] Collins, Jim *Good To Great,* New York: HarperCollins Publishers, 2001, pg. 164

[5] Ibid., pg. 165

over because it doesn't have the balancing female energy to push it up and over the top to complete the rotation. Therefore, the flywheel effect can only happen through the interaction of Yin and Yang.

When Yang works alone or is dominant, as is the case in most workplaces, its energy creates upward motion and we cheer telling ourselves we are getting results. The higher up we push it, the better our results. But, then at some point, without Yin pushing it over the top, it comes crashing down. Its momentum causes it to swing upward in the opposite direction only to only come crashing back down again. Yang energy working by itself doesn't create a flywheel, it creates pendulum swings.

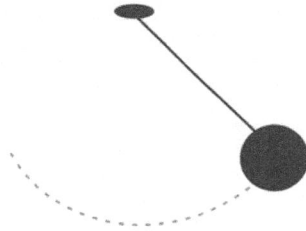

Our favor of Yang energy has conditioned us to accept pendulum swings as normal. We even think this is how balance is achieved. Worse yet, some workplaces get addicted to the drama of the highs and the subsequent crashes. These workplaces then become dysfunctional.

For the good of our workplaces and society we have to stop the pendulum swings and create the natural and gentle interaction of Yin and Yang. This of course requires empowering Yin and asserting our natural behaviors we were told were wrong, inferior and unsuitable for the workplace. It also means we must stop emulating men. When women adopt male behaviors and empower more Yang energy we drive our workplaces and society further out of balance. We make everything even worse which goes against our principle of supporting the greater common good.

Most of us have never experienced working in wholeness because our society, our workplaces, academia, media and technology are still deeply entrenched in the superiority of Yang. Therefore, we haven't experienced the new reality wholeness creates.

When we work in wholeness we see our connection to others, to something larger than ourselves and to the result of our actions. Therefore to feel good about ourselves we must see goodness, high performance and achievement coming from our action. This is connection between ourselves and the result is how wholeness inspires both men and women to support the greater common good.

Chapter 7
Pink, Blue and Purple

The first challenge women face in lifting up our half of the sky is figuring out what we should be lifting up. The characteristics traditionally associated with women aren't suitable for advancing women or creating great achievements. But then we don't want to copy men either. So, what are women's natural characteristics that we can assert to bring value to our workplace and make it whole?

Emotional   Insecure

Unintelligent   Sensitive

Dependent   Weak   Creative

Timid

Content   Being   Cooperative

Appreciative   Passive   Yielding

Receptive   Intuitive   Inward

I began my journey of answering that question when I attended a leadership workshop. During the workshop we did a session with personality testing. As the facilitator handed out the results, he described the first person, "This person likes to be all things to all people." I immediately thought, "Well, that's certainly not me," so I slouched back in my chair and zoned out. The next thing I knew he is standing in front of me. I was horrified. All I could think about was how all of my male colleagues would now see me as a stereotypical woman who needs constant validation and runs around asking everyone, "Am I doing okay?"

Completely freaked, I knew I had to figure this out. I thought about how I acted at work. I realized the test reflected how I went around from colleague to colleague coordinating their work. I kept track of where each of my colleagues was on their individual tasks and whenever there was conflict between tasks, I got my colleagues together to figure out how the tasks integrated. I had assumed the role of the big picture manager for so long that now, it was completely second nature to me.

I took on this role because I watched entropy (disorder and random errors) take over every project in my male-dominated workplaces. There was a direct correlation between the amount of entropy and the length of the project - the longer my male colleagues worked on a project, the more entropy increased. As time went on less and less energy was spent on productive work and more energy was wasted fixing problems that seemed preventable. This high level of entropy and the subsequent chaos and crisis management, made it nearly impossible to completely finish a project. However, if I asserted myself as the big picture manager and coordinated their work throughout the project, the entropy was counteracted.

Right from the start it was obvious to me that the root cause of the entropy was too much independent behavior – each of my male colleagues was in his own world, doing his own thing, his own way. They all liked working this way. To me it was weird and I felt the excessive maleness dripping from the walls of my workplaces. It reminded me of an ancient Greek phrase I learned in high school, "Nothing in Excess." That clicked. All of my workplaces had an excess of male energy and I deliberately asserted certain behaviors to balance it. Since I was the only woman and the only one using these behaviors in my workplaces, I concluded that these behaviors were inherently female.

I sat down and thought about how my male colleagues worked in each of my workplaces. I considered if I did something to balance their behavior. I began making lists. Over many years and many male-dominated workplaces, I noticed there was amazing consistency. The men used the same behaviors driven by the same characteristics in all of my workplaces. I suddenly realized I spent my entire career fixing the same problem over and over and over again.

Since there was so much consistency, I wondered if these characteristics were inherent to just my industries so I broadened my perspective. I began seeing the same characteristics everywhere. When I managed a very ethnically and culturally diverse workplace, the male behaviors weren't only the same, they were intensified.

Since the male behaviors in my lists were consistent and came from the pure male-dominated workplace they appear to be natural to men. Personally, I believe most of these characteristics are natural, but a few are nurtured by our culture and trained into men. There were some dysfunctional behaviors that I kept off my lists because I knew the men who used them dealt with abuse, alcoholism or drug addiction. I wanted to avoid the common mistake of using the behaviors of a few dysfunctional men to paint the entire male-dominated workplace because this is how we wind up with erroneous narratives.

As with the male characteristics, the female characteristics on my list reflect what I used and also saw other women in traditional roles use. The one female characteristic that is highly influenced by our culture is Abstracts in Action. Too often we cross out the "in Action" and make the characteristic just Abstracts because our culture teaches us that Action is a male characteristic.

Women's Abstracts reflect the classic female stereotypes that have no tangible value to the male-dominated workplace. They are derived from emotions such as caring, empathy, compassion and sensitivity. When women espouse these Abstracts in the workplace, men send us off to sit in a circle, hold hands and sing inspirational songs. They remain of little value and do nothing to support the greater common good unless we choose to put them into Action.

Male and Female Balancing Characteristics

BLUE ZONE	PURPLE ZONE	PINK ZONE
Autonomy	Teamwork	Group
Tangibles in Action		Abstracts in Action
Task Expertise	Leadership	Multiple Task Management
Done!		Done Well
Linear Perspective	Systems Thinking	Circular Perspective
Ego Protection		Dispensable Ego
Stress Limits	Sustained High Performance	Stress Endurance
Power Over Change		Adapt to Change
Offensively Aggressive	Continuous Improvement	Defensively Aggressive
Energy Restraint		Energy Projection

In keeping with tradition, I used Pink to represent female characteristics and Blue to represent male characteristics. A workplace that has an excess of the female characteristics is out of balance and inefficient because it operates in the Pink Zone. Likewise, a workplace that has an excess of male characteristics is out of balance and inefficient because it operates in the Blue Zone. We expect workplaces that have predominantly male employees and managers to be in the Blue Zone. However, workplaces that are predominantly female can also be in the Blue Zone. This is the effect of the Doctrine of Two Spheres, the stereotypes and a feminist movement that encourages women to embrace male characteristics. Women can also be in the Blue Zone simply because our jobs were originally filled or designed by men and men instructed us on how to do the job.

The Blue Zone and the Pink Zone each function as a system with the characteristics reinforcing each other but predominantly reinforcing the primary characteristic and its guiding principle. In the Blue Zone, the primary male characteristic is Autonomy and the guiding principle is belief in the power of the individual.

Autonomy and the power of the individual give us the self-made man, the conquering hero, the wise father figure and the Philosopher-King. My favorite explanation of the power of the individual comes from the title of the first chapter of Peter Senge's book *The Fifth Discipline*. It is titled: "Give Me A Lever Long Enough…And Single-Handed I Can Move The World."[6]

That is the Blue Zone in a nutshell.

Our workplaces demonstrate their support for Autonomy and their belief in the power of the individual with statements such as "Our People Make The Difference" or "Only The Best and The Brightest Work Here." They endorse teamwork, but believe the best team is comprised of A-players. After a goal or objective is achieved, they single out one individual as the MVP.

Blue Zone workplaces believe it is the power of the individual that makes things happen and brings success. It believes the "right individual" has the answers and knows what to do. It attributes corporate success to the personality of an individual CEO such as

---

[6] Senge, Peter *The Fifth Discipline The Art & Practice of The Learning Organization*, New York: Doubleday, 1990, pg. 3

Henry Ford, Jack Welch, Lee Iacocca, Steve Jobs, Bill Gates, Elon Musk or Richard Branson. We are taught this as a "truth." However, it is really pure Blue Zone thinking.

As women we don't realize how much we've been indoctrinated into Blue Zone thinking and how many of the "truths" we are taught come from the Blue Zone. As you grow your understanding of each of the Blue Zone characteristics you will be amazed at how deeply immersed in the Blue Zone and Yang energy our society and workplaces are. You will see Blue and especially Autonomy everywhere. When you are able to recognize Blue behavior you can begin to break free of your Blue Zone indoctrination and come into your own inherent power.

Given that Autonomy is men's primary characteristic we assume Group is the primary female characteristic and stronger together is our guiding principle. That is our logical and rational conclusion because Group is the opposite of Autonomy. It also fits the narrative we've always heard about how primitive men were lone hunters while women stayed back in the village in female groups to prepare food and care for children. But the real reason we conclude Group is the primary female characteristic is because that is what our Blue Zone indoctrination taught us. Making Group the primary female characteristic reinforces our belief in the power of the individual and the superiority of Yang and male energy.

From our own experiences we know that when we work in groups or in teams, it is difficult to get everyone to agree, work together and move in the same direction in unison. Therefore, a group needs a strong and powerful leader. The leader separates himself from the Group, stands out in front by himself, decides what the Group should do and directs the Group in the execution of his decisions. This elevates the Autonomy of an individual above the Group; the Blue Zone above the Pink Zone and covertly reinforces the superiority of male over female. This is how Blue Zone indoctrination works to mask the fact that we aren't working in wholeness.

It took a while for me to break free of my Blue Zone indoctrination too but when I did, I came to realize the primary Pink Zone characteristic is Energy Projection and our guiding principle is supporting the greater common good.

When I first made my lists, Energy Projection represented how women were social and planned the social events in my workplaces. Men's corresponding Energy Restraint represented how many of my male colleagues were always noncommittal about attending social events unless there was free food and beer. This seemed trivial, so I almost left these characteristics off my list which is literally why they are at the bottom.

However my perspective changed when I began exploring why I felt so drained by my male-dominated workplaces. I knew there was more to it than just long hours and the stress of trying to meet construction deadlines and financial goals. There was something about working with the men that was literally exhausting.

I realized the Blue Zone is a huge energy consumer because it takes a lot of energy to overcome all of the entropy to actually complete the work. In all my workplaces the men could complete about 95% of their work, but getting that last 5% done was an enormous challenge. Consequently, my male colleagues were restrained in their energy and used their characteristic of Done! to declare that 95% completion was good enough. It kept them from the intense stress and the myriad of health issues brought on by trying to reach 100%. It was their survival technique.

As I watched the women in some of my more exhausting workplaces I realized that women distanced themselves from men or worked in close contact with other women. It was our survival technique against the men who need to steal female energy to recharge themselves so they can continue working in the Blue Zone. For me, it explained why I often thought of some of my male colleagues as leeches sucking the life blood out of me.

After one particular project left me feeling tired and drained, I wanted to reconnect myself to my feminine energy so I joined some women's groups in my community. I am fortunate to live in a town that accepts alternative and non-conventional lifestyles so it embraces female energy. I was immediately struck by the stark difference between the male energy of my workplaces and the female energy of my groups. I left my meetings feeling happy and energized.

A while later when I read about True Womanhood's belief that women shine a bright light out into the world, I was immediately reminded of my experience with the women's groups. In all of my groups, we expelled our negativity, connected with something larger than ourselves (based on our individual beliefs) and drew in its positive energy. After meetings, we projected positive energy and shared it with the outside world.

There seems to be something inherently natural about women projecting positivity, shining a bright light out into the world and supporting the greater common good. It is an inherent part of womanhood that women carried with them throughout the ages that modern women have lost touch with. Without this vital part of ourselves, we can feel empty inside just like the suburban housewives of the 1950s and 60s. When we don't make it a part of our definition of workplace success we aren't inspired to climb the workplace hierarchy and achieve all we can. Today, as we look at all the negative energy being created around us, we realize how much we need to reconnect with this part of ourselves and lift up our half of the sky.

Chapter 8
Stay Out of the Blue Zone

All of us are taught to go into the Blue Zone. However after decades of working with men, the hardest, been there - done that - this is what worked, lesson I learned is:

Stay out of the Blue Zone!

Never, ever, ever go into the Blue Zone. Other women who haven't worked in an all-male workplace will foolishly advise you to get into the Blue Zone so you can compete with men. Your male colleagues will bait you and lure you into the Blue Zone. Don't go there.

I know from personal experience just how hard it is to stay out of the Blue Zone when everyone else you work with is in there. It is so easy to get sucked in especially when you get frustrated. When this happens we need to make an immediate U-turn and get out.

We must remember that the Blue Zone is all about empowering male behaviors, especially Autonomy. When we adopt behaviors that aren't natural to us, we become very unhappy. We can go home at the end of the day not liking our job and not wanting to go back. I've worked with a few women who fully embraced Autonomy and became the Bluest person in their workplace. They were the most miserable and unhappy women I've ever known.

We also have to be completely honest with ourselves about how successful we can actually be by working in the Blue Zone. The vast majority of us aren't going to advance in the workplace by competing with men on their terms or by trying to out-man all the men in our workplace. Nor are we going to distinguish ourselves by achieving something bigger and better. Our male-dominated workplaces are already full of male energy and horribly out of balance so, the last thing it needs is us adding to the imbalance.

With all that said, the biggest reason we need to stay out of the Blue Zone is simply because we don't understand it.

So many of our narratives about how the male-dominated workplace functions were written while we stood within the private sphere and gazed off into the distant public sphere. From our vantage point we believed we were watching the male proving ground where survival of the fittest played out and the strongest man rose to the top. The public sphere was where our powerful ideal men – the type of men we needed to attach ourselves to for our own power and status – were produced. We saw the public sphere through the lens of what we needed it to be and concluded that the male-dominated workplace thrives on competition, aggression and intimidation in a quest for power over others.

Armed with our perceptions, we entered the male-dominated workplace ready to fight men for our place at the top. We deployed the tactic "tear-down-to-rise-up," believing that if we were aggressive enough, we could pull down the patriarchal good ole boys hierarchy, climb the corporate ladder and take power for ourselves. Once we seized our power, we could finally have control over our lives, the lives of men and the power to mold society.

As we expected, men responded aggressively to us. They didn't want to give up their power. Their response confirmed to us that the male-dominated workplace thrives on competition and aggression and power is its ultimate prize. However, our conclusion was merely a self-fulfilling prophecy and far from accurate. This is why we haven't advanced.

In the Blue Zone men don't aspire to have power over others. They aspire to prevent others from having power over them. There is a huge difference between the two which women haven't understood.

When no one has power over you, you have complete self-determination and Autonomy. You are free to do what you want, when you want, how you want. You don't have to ask anyone else's permission or answer to anyone else for what you do.

Autonomy is men's natural source of empowerment. Once a man turns 18 and becomes a legal adult, he sees himself as 100% empowered to act on his own authority. To limit his Autonomy, he requires laws, rules and policies that are enforced. So, unless something explicitly limits him, a man assumes he is empowered to act according to what he believes is best. In our workplaces we hear men express this with the statement: "It is better to ask for forgiveness than for permission." To men, asking for permission is something a child does, not an adult.

When women went into the male-dominated workplace and deployed tear-down-to-rise-up, men interpreted our actions as an attack on their Autonomy – as us trying to have power over them. They instinctively fought back to protect their Autonomy but we didn't recognize it for what it was. This is the mistake we've been making for decades.

We mistakenly assumed men had the same relationship with power as we did. Because a century ago we had no power or legal rights we needed laws, rules and policies to give us power. Our history told us that power isn't inherent to us; it is fought for and granted by those who have power. Unfortunately, we continue to think this way and in doing so we create imaginary barriers.

Whenever women feel like we aren't empowered enough we want more laws, rules and policies to grant us power. In other words we still think like teenagers who have to ask Mom and Dad for additional privileges. Men see us doing this and it influences their perceptions of us.

Today there is no reason why we shouldn't have the same perspective about our empowerment and right to self-determination as men. We should assume that once we become legal adults we are fully empowered to act on our own authority. We then need laws, rules and policies to limit our Autonomy. So unless there is something explicitly limiting us, we should assume we are empowered to act according to what we believe is best. It is amazing how many barriers just dissipate as soon as you stop giving people power over you.

Believing in our own empowerment and our own right to self-determination is the most important lesson I learned from being the woman in the room, listening to the advice men give other men. Never once in my career did I ever think that I wasn't just as empowered as my male colleagues or that I wasn't their complete equal. That is why it took me so long to realize that being a woman made me different from my male colleagues and contributed to my success.

Of course, there are some controlling, oppressive and authoritarian men in the workplace. We think these men prize power for nefarious reasons but in my experience most of them are just very insecure. They believe everyone else is diminishing their Autonomy so they try to control everyone else's actions in order to regain their Autonomy. However, they forget that in the Blue Zone, Autonomy is a natural neutralizer of power, oppression and control. (Many men pulled me aside and explained to me exactly how this works.)

When a group of men are oppressed by an authoritarian, they interpret it as being treated like a child by an overbearing father. They need to feel like adults again so they reassert their Autonomy by scattering in all different directions and disappearing. During their disappearance they do whatever they want, the way they want. Each man will disappear for as long as it takes for him to feel like he has regained his self-determination. This creates a rampage of chaos and regaining control is worse than herding cats. I've watched many groups of men successfully use massive amounts of Autonomy to take down oppressive and authoritarian men. They don't use tear-down-to-rise-up.

Because we haven't understood the importance of Autonomy, we've given way too much importance and power to hierarchal power in the male-dominated workplace. Consequently, we are being counterproductive to our causes. We are teaching men new behaviors that negatively impact our ability to advance in the male-dominated workplace.

In the beginning of my career when men were frustrated and stressed at work, they yelled, screamed and cursed a lot. However, most men were still gentlemanly and respectful towards women, often apologizing for their emotional outbursts in the presence of a woman. Their behavior stemmed from women using the power of "No" and expecting men to elevate their behavior around women. However, feminists saw it as men treating women differently which automatically meant it was demeaning behavior. They chastised men for being gentlemen. So, men stopped.

The long term consequence was that men didn't change how men interacted with each other, but they changed how they interact with women – we gave men permission to be the ugliest version of themselves with us. Today, many younger men (Gen X and Millennials) are mean and openly bully women. They use tear-down-and-demean against us, making their behavior today much worse than anything I experienced back in the 20th century when my male colleagues were still expected to be gentlemen.

Women have to question what role we played in creating this change by deploying our erroneous narratives that encouraged women to use Yang energy in workplaces that were already deeply Blue.

- Did we teach younger men that the male-dominated workplace functions through power, control and intimidation when dealing with women?

- Is the reason some women treat each other worse than men because we taught women to go into the Blue Zone and use tear-down-to-rise-up on each other?
- Does our perceived lack of empowerment and right to self-determination perpetuate paternalism by telling men to treat us as teenagers who need their adult permission?
- Are we encouraging dysfunctional workplace behavior?

As women, must understand Autonomy and how it drives the male-dominated workplace. We must understand that to men Autonomy is power and extreme Blue Zone behavior produces Autonomotarians, not Authoritarians or Autocrats. Extremely Blue behavior materializes as selfishness, greed and a Me-First or Me-Only attitude. The deepest Blue workplace I experienced wasn't at all aggressive, intimidating, combative or oppressive. It was overrun by selfish men who didn't care about the workplace. They only cared about "what works best for me" as they used and abused the workplace for personal gain. They had no regard for what was fair, right, moral or ethical.

In the deepest, darkest depths of the Blue Zone, men's belief in the power of the individual and their Power Over Change gets out of control. Men put on blinders and go behind the closed doors of their echo chambers where they depart from reality and believe whatever they want to happen, will happen. When their action produces unintended consequences, they respond by going deeper into the Blue Zone believing they have to divine power to bend reality to their will. In these dark depths, people (men and women) cross ethical and legal lines. It is the most destructive behavior in the workplace.

Women who support the greater common good have the power to stop excessive and destructive Blue Zone behavior. And our male colleagues would love it if we could.

Women don't know it, but men have a big secret - they hate the Blue Zone as much as women. Maybe, even more.

The Blue Zone's chaos, volatile pendulum swings and unpredictable consequences create a frustrating, stressful, energy consuming environment where going to work is like pounding your head against a brick wall all day. This environment leads to abusive behavior, alcoholism, drug addiction and a myriad of health issues. The only men who like the Blue Zone are the selfish few who are in it for personal gain and believe a big reward is imminent.

The truth is the vast majority of our male colleagues would gladly leave the Blue Zone. However, they have no idea how or even that it is possible, so they remain trapped. Their only hope is that women finally empower ourselves, lift up our half of the sky and re-write our fairytale:

> Once upon a time, poor countrymen tended their fields barely providing enough food for their families. Then one day a stranger approached and told them of the magnificent Blue Zone city that promised them great wealth if they worked in its factories. So, off the men went. After a few days, the men realized they had been tricked. They wanted to leave but they couldn't open the doors. They were trapped inside. Many years went by and eventually men lost all hope ever leaving.
>
> Then one day, some women came to the city and saw the factory. They asked an old peasant what it was. He told them about the factory and of the men who toiled long hours inside. The women knew this wasn't right and the men needed to be freed. They mounted their white horses and valiantly set out at once. As they approached, the gates and doors of the factory swung open on their own and let the women pass. The men stared in amazement and said, "Is it you? Are you the ones we have waited for so long to rescue us?"
>
> The women told them they were and gathered the men on their horses. The women rode the men out through the darkness of the Blue Zone city and into the bright sunshine of a new beautiful land. The men had never seen anything so

beautiful before. They asked, "What do you call this land?" The women replied "It is the Purple Zone." The men and women dismounted their horses and the men began to discover everything they were promised in the Blue Zone, but never received. From that day forward, men and women tended to the Purple Zone in full equality as they worked together happily ever after.

Chapter 9
The Purple Zone

When women assert our female characteristics into a Blue Zone workplace, we blend our Pink characteristics into the workplace's Blue characteristics and transform it. We create the Purple Zone.

Pink + Blue = Purple

The Purple Zone is where our workplace achieves harmony, balance and wholeness. To achieve the Purple Zone men and women must interact and influence each other just as Yin and Yang energies do. This interaction puts the whole into motion. Therefore, a Purple Zone workplace isn't static or one monochromatic shade of Purple. It is fluid and dynamic, encompassing the full spectrum of Purple as it changes shades in response to varying, issues, conditions and situations. A workplace can be indigo when more male characteristics are needed and lavender when more female characteristics are needed.

In order for men and women to continuously interact and influence each other there must be men and women across all roles and management levels. Our workplaces can't achieve wholeness when its employees are divided by gender with men in senior management, sales and operations and women in administration, human resources, marketing and book-keeping. We have to recognize that all positions benefit from the influence of the non-traditional gender.

People should also work in shades of Purple and strive to grow characteristics complementary to their own. If we look at Yin-Yang symbol we notice the Yin and Yang each has a part of the other within them. This is how men and women achieve balance and wholeness within themselves. People who can flow through a broad spectrum of Purple have wider perspectives and find it easier to see what is missing in our workplaces and what characteristics it needs. We can then fill that need ourselves or find the right person who can. Too often we are encouraged to fit in and be like everyone else. But a workplace where everyone is always trying to think the same be one monochromatic shade of Purple will under-perform.

Since our workplaces and institutions dismiss female characteristics as trivial, they know very little about the Pink Zone and its benefits. Therefore, it is up to women to assert our characteristics and teach men their value. Like it or not, it is our responsibility to lead men to the Purple Zone.

Stepping up and leading our male-dominated workplaces can seem daunting because our definitions of teamwork and leadership stem from our Blue Zone indoctrination. They tell us influence and change can only happen when directed from the top down. But the truth is, Autonomy ensures top-down directed change fails and the male-dominated workplace knows it. This is why the lowliest woman in admin who uses Purple Zone Teamwork and Leadership has more power to affect change than the CEO.

Using Purple Zone Teamwork and Leadership we start the flywheel slowly rotating. This puts the whole into motion and our static, fragmented way of working begins to fade away. As the flywheel rotates we build a system by connecting and integrating more people, functions, tasks and information. As we integrate more pieces into the system, the flywheel spins faster. The whole is put into motion by working through systems.

Whether we recognize it or not, all of us work within a system. We receive an item or information from our customers or co-workers then, we perform our task on it before we pass it off for someone else to work on. Collectively we are a team and we create the system our workplace uses to produce its product or service. The system we create is more valuable to accomplishing our workplace's objectives than the most powerful of individuals.

Looking back I realize I first discovered the Purple Zone during the second year of my career. As a typical 2nd Lieutenant I was assigned the projects no one else wanted. For one of my projects I had to train my squadron's team for a big Air Force competition, the Olympic Arena. To the base leadership, this competition was a huge deal, but within my squadron it was considered a pure waste of time. Out of all the yearly assignments, this was considered the worst of the worst.

Normally, a squadron would assign only their best and most experienced people to represent them in the competition. But because of my squadron's attitude, I got the two least experienced airmen for my team – one man and one woman, both younger than me who were just a few months out of tech school. None of us knew anything about how to do the competition task.

I asked for a more senior person to help us and he was assigned. However, he didn't show up. To make matters worse, we were openly mocked every day when we went to train. We were told we were wasting time when there was so much real work to do. It was demoralizing.

We fumbled around for over a month. Then I overheard someone joke that the Air Force was so uptight that it had a technical order (TO) and checklist for everything. That gave me an idea – there was probably a TO for our task. I found it and read it. From there I wrote out a flow chart or process to take us through our task.

Over the next 6 weeks we trained using our process. As we changed scenarios we learned more and kept refining our process. Our process wasn't like the checklists the Air Force loved because my team used process to think their way through the scenarios. They made minor adjustments and solved problems on the fly all while using the right tools for the task at hand. By the time they left for the competition they felt very confident.

When they arrived at the competition they were immediately laughed at. Within hours they were nicknamed "The Kindergartners." They were 12 years junior to the next most junior competitor who was glad to see them arrive and replace him as the brunt of jokes. Most of their competitors had over 20 years of experience. My male team member was competing against his tech school instructor and my female team member was the only woman and the first to ever compete.

By the end of the day everyone knew who my team was including a powerful four-star general. Late that night he called our Wing Commander to question his judgement for allowing "The Kindergartners" to represent him. Rumors quickly circulated that my team could cost our Wing Commander his job.

The next day, after my team competed I asked them how they did. They said they thought they did just fine. Remarkably they said they weren't at all nervous during the competition.

On the night of the awards ceremony, my base was disappointed as other base teams lost. Finally it was time for the Civil Engineering award. Everyone immediately moved away from me, distancing themselves for what they knew was going to be a humiliating loss. One person even gave me the sympathetic "It's been nice knowing you, your career is over" look.

As the announcer prepared to announce the winning team, he said they had the highest score in the entire competition, scoring an almost perfect 194 out of 200 points. The winner was – My Team!

In the absolute stunned dead silence the only sound was me jumping to me feet and yelling "YEAH" at the top of my lungs.

Our process proved to be almost perfect. They made only one mistake on the one issue we knew we weren't sure about.

We weren't like all the other competition teams who followed the Blue Zone rules by believing in the power of the knowledge and experience of individual team members. Instead we violated every Blue Zone rule and in doing so should have failed miserably. But since we competed from the Purple Zone, we won.

After that competition, I never cared that I didn't have the best and the brightest, the most experienced or the most educated personnel on my teams. I never care about gender, race, religion or any of that stuff. I never care what they wore, what color their hair was, how piercing they had or where they were tattooed. I only cared that my team members were willing to think and learn.

Throughout my career, I took my teams of thinkers and learners and turned them into complex problem solvers simply by giving them permission to do so. That was all the empowerment they needed. Together we figured out all the processes and systems we needed to do our work. As we used our systems, we discovered new problems so we used our problem solving skills to figure out what was wrong. Together we improved and refined our processes. In a matter of a few months our performance soared. By using Purple Zone Teamwork, Leadership and Systems-Thinking, we created our high-performing, high-achieving Purple Zone workplace.

Chapter 10
Complexity – Our BFF

Over the past few decades the world has changed dramatically - everything has gotten more complex. We can hardly discuss a problem or an issue without using the word "complex" to describe why we struggle to resolve it. Too often we think we have the solution figured out, only to find that when we implement our solution, a whole new crop of problems pop up. We call this the Law of Unintended Consequences and tell ourselves that they couldn't have been foreseen or prevented. We use Complexity as an excuse but in the back our mind we know the truth - they could have been foreseen and prevented. We just didn't know how to go about seeing them in advance.

Out of all the challenges my workplaces faced, managing Complexity was at the top. Their solution was to request more money, more people or better computer systems. Even if all of these requests were granted, problems endured. So, my workplaces went deeper into the Blue Zone and threw more people at the problem. They were searching for that one man who had all the right skills to make the problems magically go away. However, he was never found.

Why a person or even team of highly skilled people can't prevent or solve complex problems requires us to understand what we are missing in our current problem solving methodology. The construction industry gives us a great example to learn from.

Many years ago, in an effort to improve performance the industry introduced a method called Design-Build. It was supposed to harken us back to the simpler days of construction when we had master-builders. The industry cited how centuries ago, if you wanted a ship built, you went to a master ship-builder. He knew everything there is to know about building a ship. The master ship-builder designed your ship and then with the help of a couple of apprentices, built your ship.

This of course is a pure Blue Zone solution. Design-Build tries to side-step Complexity by harkening us back to the glory days when the power of the individual was all we needed. It ignores that today's ships are larger and require several specialized skills. One master-builder can't possibly know every detail and direct hundreds of people in the design and construction of a ship. But by using the term master-builder the industry tries to trick itself into thinking Complexity can be managed through simplification. It is reminiscent of how the Blue Zone tells us not to look at all the trees, but at just 1 forest.

In practice a master-builder isn't a single person or a single company. Like a forest it is a complex entity comprised of many smaller and diverse entities:

- A general contractor
- An architectural firm
- Engineering firms in various disciplines
- Material suppliers
- Equipment suppliers
- Subcontractors in every trade

This adds up to about 50 different entities, each of which is comprised of many individuals. All together, these individuals complete thousands of tasks. That's a lot of pieces that have to come together just right to construct a structure that will function as intended. Our struggle with Complexity is how to efficiently and effectively bring all of those thousands of pieces together in the shortest amount of time and with the least amount of wasted money.

I wondered how the construction industry recommended we accomplish this so I pulled out my notes from a design-build training course. There were several slides devoted to teaming and the need to make the mental shift to a cooperative team approach. But for all of the discussion, the presentation didn't say how to make the mental shift to a cooperative team approach, only that it needed to be done.

From my experience I knew exactly why it couldn't say how to make the mental shift – because it doesn't know how.

I've heard the male-dominated workplace discuss its need to make mind shifts and paradigm shifts since the 1980s. I've watched it go through all kinds of gyrations to try to achieve these shifts and ultimately produce very little change. The problem is that the male-dominated workplace doesn't instinctively know what a cooperative team approach is. It isn't a behavior men endeavor to learn or adopt because it is in direct conflict with Autonomy. Therefore workplaces that stay in the Blue Zone and immersed in Autonomy struggle to effectively manage Complexity.

Women on the other hand, instinctively know what a cooperative team approach is because it is rooted in Pink Zone characteristics. In the Purple Zone its shade would be something like orchid, very close to the Pink end of the spectrum.

To implement a cooperative team approach requires changing the focus from just what needs to get done to also asking how it gets done. It requires understanding the relationships between all the pieces and how they have to be integrated to accomplish our larger objective.

With greater focus on the relationships and integration, whenever a piece acts, the other pieces perk up to see if they are also affected. For example, in construction if there is a design change to framing, it may impact the foundation, plumbing, electrical, mechanical, insulation, roofing, drywall, painting, flooring, equipment rental, safety, contracts, insurance and billing. All of these impacts means there is a high degree of integration between the pieces. This is what increases Complexity.

Imagine what happens if the design change to framing is made autonomously and no one else is notified of the change. Now imagine what happens when other people make similar autonomous decisions during the day. Many of our workplaces function like this and we don't realize it because we are taught to accept it as standard operating procedure. But if we become aware of it and stop it, we can eliminate chronic waste, chaos and unintended consequences.

In order to also focus on how to get things done, Complexity demands that Yin energy and female characteristics take their rightful place. She demands that Yin and Yang, male and female characteristics work in full equality in the Purple Zone or face the consequences. So far, our Blue Zone workplaces aren't doing a very good job of listening to her. They believe they can ignore Complexity or pass her off to technology to manage. But Complexity won't allow herself to be dismissed, subjugated or discarded.

Complexity is the ultimate bitch. She knows men hold up only half the sky and she has no qualms about reminding them of that fact every chance she gets. Anyone who doesn't give her the respect she is due will feel her wrath. When angered she bitch-slaps our workplaces bringing the pendulum crashing down, wreaking havoc with waves of unintended consequences. She creates crises that plunge us into the depths of chaos. As a society we've experienced her wrath many times this century:

- The dot-com collapse
- The horrible response to Hurricane Katrina
- Terrorism
- Failed Middle East interventions
- The housing crash
- The Great Recession
- Computer system hacking
- Healthcare

Personally, I spent a few years working on "The Project from Hell." It was really a group of integrated projects where Complexity wasn't properly managed and went on a wild rampage. I joined the project in its second year and equated resolving the unintended consequences to trying to untangle the knots in a massive mangled ball of yarn. Autonomy remained rampant until I asserted my female characteristics and expanded my role which didn't sit well with a couple of managers. At first, I fought back but then Complexity tapped me on the shoulder and said, "I got this." She continued to wreak havoc and in doing so created numerous opportunities for me to reassert myself. On our little team Complexity played the bitch while I got to be the heroine who kept coming up with the solutions to the problems she created. Together we went round and round with management for months until she finally broke them and I got the respect and recognition I deserved.

It was on this project that I first proved to myself that being a woman made all the difference. When another woman finally joined the project we joined forces and together proved how well women work with Complexity as we quickly finished the largest part of the project by ourselves.

The bottom line is that Complexity has changed everything and all of us (both men and women) need to accept that. Gone are the days where Yang energy and Blue Zone characteristics are enough for success. As one half of the whole they are insufficient to produce the complete solutions to the issues and problems Complexity now throws at us.

Complexity is requiring women lift up our half of the sky and take our rightful place in the world. She negated and removed all of the excuses we like to use as to why we can't. She is an ardent feminist who took over blazing the trail to advance women and made it a paved road. She will continue to do more to advance women than any new law, rule or policy could ever hope to achieve. She is our BFF and believes in what we can make happen. We need to accept her friendship and let her work on our behalf.

The truth is it's not just men who need to make the mental shift – women need to make it too. We must believe that who we are, is not only valuable, but critical to workplace success in the complex 21st century and beyond.

Chapter 11
Womens 21st Century
Super Power

Sometime in the past your workplace probably instituted a new initiative and declared it would become systems-driven. They may have called it TQM, LEAN or Six Sigma. As part of the initiative, senior management wrote a Mission Statement and its list of Core Values. They announced they would standardize all company procedures and purchased new management software. If your workplace didn't have one already, it created a Quality Department to lead the standardization effort.

Even though your workplace didn't advertise it as such, this initiative was an attempt to reign in Autonomy and that is how everyone interpreted it. Employees rebelled, declaring that their situation was special or unique and standardized procedures would not work for them. They threw up road blocks making their resistance difficult to overcome. Eventually the initiative faded away and for the most part everyone went back to doing their work the same way they always had. The systems-driven workplace was added to the long list of failed initiatives to propel the male-dominated workplace to better performance.

I was at the forefront of creating systems-driven workplaces having gotten involved right after my success with the Air Force Olympic Arena competition. I discovered I was really good at it. My male colleagues however were lost and confused. As I got more involved, I kept hearing the experts express their frustration about how difficult it was for workplaces "to make the necessary paradigm shift" that would move them away from their traditional practices to thinking in terms of systems. I was baffled as to why men thought this was so hard.

At first, I attributed my success to being an engineer and particularly to a systems engineering course I took my freshman year in college. But then, I realized many of the people who were struggling were engineers who also studied systems engineering in college. So, even though I couldn't explain why, I knew the problem was a man-thing.

The real reason men struggle to create a systems-driven workplace because they try to do it in the Blue Zone, without any Yin or female characteristics. They apply massive amounts of Yang. They make systems all technical and engineeringie; full of rational scientific and statistical analytics logically presented in linear graphs and charts so they can objectively deduce what is happening and develop a 10 point plan to correct it. This Yang overload drives Complexity crazy.

Complexity has a problem with men because they simply don't understand that systems are pure Purple and systems driven workplaces only exist in the Purple Zone. In his book, Peter Senge probably unknowingly, suggests this too. In one short, easily missed sentence he writes, "Systems thinking is a discipline for seeing wholes."[7]

As soon as we see the word "whole," the alarms in our heads should sound. We should immediately think of male and female interaction. This clues us in to understand that in order for men to make their critical paradigm shift to systems thinking they need women beside them asserting our Pink Zone characteristics.

---

[7] Senge, Peter *The Fifth Discipline The Art & Practice of The Learning Organization*, New York: Doubleday, 1990, pg. 68

However, we've never been told we need to do this. Instead we get loads of Blue Zone propaganda that tells us systems are Blue and require Blue Zone thinking.

Given the amount of Blue Zone propaganda we are fed, it is no wonder that women are turned off by the true systems driven professions such as technology, medicine, engineering, logistics, construction, manufacturing and science as well as many of the skilled labor trades. Men take these industries that are naturally dynamic, interesting and fun and make it static, boring and Blue. Complexity says it's time for us to stop believing this Blue Zone propaganda and to rescue these professions from their Blue Zone captivity. But to do so, we first have to understand and recognize the Blue Zone thinking we are taught as truths.

Blue Zone thinking focuses too much on the pieces/tasks to create Tangible Action. When the Blue Zone's Autonomy and Tangible Action combine with its Linear Perspective, the Blue Zone sees an Action creating a Result. This one-to-one correlation negates any need to understand or define the relationship between the Action and the Result.

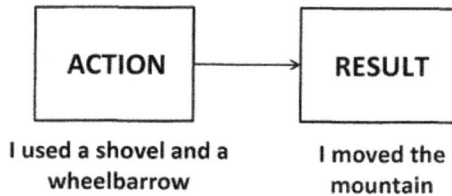

| ACTION | → | RESULT |

I used a shovel and a wheelbarrow   I moved the mountain

Using a simple Cause and Effect relationship, men can simply and confidently declare:

"I took this Action and of course I got the Result I wanted."

As women we are constantly told to buy into this thinking and adopt it for ourselves. We are told it demonstrates we have the all-important confidence so critical to workplace success. I, however, learned a long time ago to never trust a highly confident man who makes these types of statements. To me, a highly confident man is a big waving red flag and the first place I look to find the source of workplace problems.

In the reality of our complex workplaces, a singular Action only produces a portion of our desired Result. By thinking in over-simplified Action and Result terms, the Blue Zone misses all of the additional Actions that are needed to create our desired Result. They can also miss the importance of how they must bring all the pieces/tasks together to get Better Results.

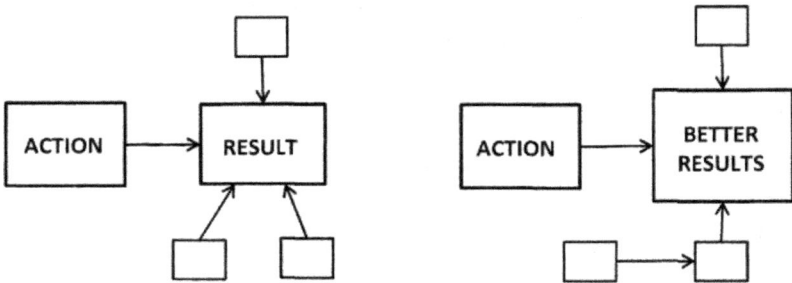

Over-simplified Action and Result is also why we have unintended consequences that diminish our Results. In my Design-Build example the framing design change had many repercussions. Each of these repercussions was an opportunity to lose time and/or money if they weren't recognized and dealt with properly.

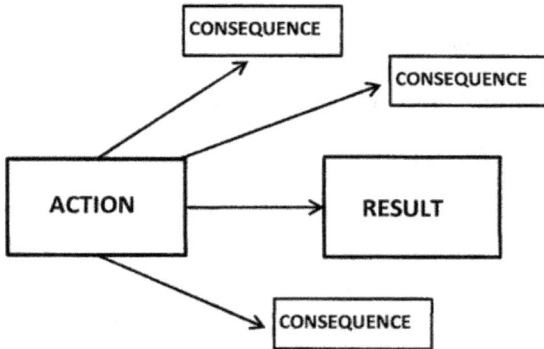

Throughout my career I continually dealt with men who took Action without realizing all of the repercussions of their Actions. I don't, however, completely blame the men because they've never been expected see the full consequences of their Action beyond their desired Result. Their own Blue Zone indoctrination prohibited them from broadening their perspective beyond the simple Action and Result scenario.

The Blue Zone also applies simple Action and Result to its large tasks. When large complex tasks are broken down into individual pieces/tasks, the whole is reassembled using the Blue Zone's Linear Perspective. It applies systematic thinking to create the step-by-step procedures we are familiar with.

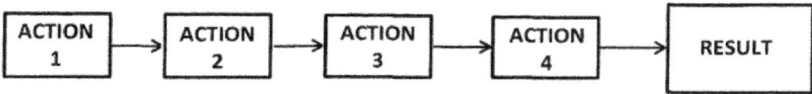

```
┌──────────┐   ┌──────────┐   ┌──────────┐   ┌──────────┐   ┌──────────┐
│ ACTION   │   │ ACTION   │   │ ACTION   │   │ ACTION   │   │          │
│   1      │──▶│   2      │──▶│   3      │──▶│   4      │──▶│  RESULT  │
└──────────┘   └──────────┘   └──────────┘   └──────────┘   └──────────┘
```

These procedures are static and inflexible so when conditions vary, the procedure produces different Results. This is what everyone intuitively understands when they rebel against management's standardized procedures.

The Blue Zone, however, doesn't want to acknowledge everyone's concerns because it doesn't know how to deal with them. So it pulls out its propaganda and tries to convince everyone that they just don't get it because they don't understand systematic thinking.

The Blue Zone loves its systematic thinking because it is clear, orderly, logical and disciplined. It believes systematic thinking contains and controls Complexity. This of course angers Complexity who detests systematic thinking for all of its inadequacies. But the Blue Zone won't listen to her because it promotes systematic thinking as the highest order of thinking.

Complexity is determined to stop the Blue Zone propaganda campaign that promotes the superiority of systematic thinking and tries to convince us it is the same as systems thinking. She is on a crusade to prove they are not the same.

Systematic thinking cannot create systems. It can however create Swiss cheese workplaces, unintended consequences, inferior performance and erroneous conclusions. All too often the Blue Zone conducts scientific studies and reaches a conclusion believing it has defined a Cause and Effect. That conclusion however, can be at odds with the conclusion of another scientific study. Or the study can fail to consider all the other things that influence the conclusion.

Inadequate thinking like this angers Complexity. She wants the studies to understand and/or define the relationship between all the Causes and the Effect. Unless they can do that she throws the study in the trash can alongside all the other scientific studies that supported the Doctrine of Two Spheres and the stereotypes.

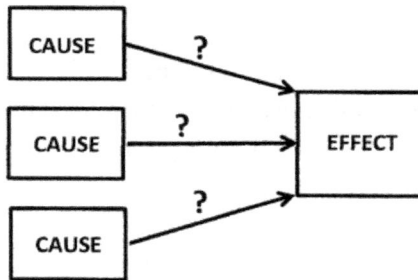

The real difference between systematic thinking and systems thinking is literally thinking. In our workplaces systematic thinking is typically done by someone we consider very smart. Because they are so smart, they plan or design the procedures the rest of the workplace will use. This gives everyone else permission to be like a 19th century factory worker who was told to park their brain and follow the procedure as dictated. But this is where Complexity likes to step in and prove what a bitch she can be. She creates a problem or changes conditions so the dictated procedure doesn't work and doesn't deliver the desired results.

Suddenly there is conflict in the workplace. Is the procedure wrong? Or, is there something wrong with the people who are implementing it? In the Blue Zone, the resolution typically follows the scenario of a lot of arguing back and forth until the people who are supposed to use the procedure get frustrated. They figure out the solution and fix the problem on their own. This makes Complexity very proud because she doesn't like systematic thinking's arrogance that presumes only a select few people are capable of its higher order of thinking.

On the other hand, Complexity loves systems thinking because it recognizes the intelligence of every team member. It acknowledges that everyone can think, plan and solve problems. Therefore, systems thinking doesn't dictate how to do a job, but rather it provides a roadmap for everyone to think their way through their jobs. This is exactly what my Air Force team did to win their competition.

Going back to what Peter Senge wrote, "Systems thinking is a discipline for seeing wholes,"[8] we realize the flaw of systematic thinking is that it substitutes Yang's order and sequencing for Yin's relationships. It doesn't recognize the value of understanding how all the pieces/tasks influence each other and need to be integrated.

Systems thinking however, values understanding the relationship between the pieces/tasks and that makes Complexity very happy. She says systems thinking should make women very happy too. It allows us to break free of the Blue Zone and its systematic thinking no matter what profession we are in. It tells women it is okay to think the way we do.

Because systems are Purple, fluid and dynamic they require our Adapt to Change and Circular Perspective in order to respond to changes in situations, conditions and environments. This gives women an advantage. Unlike men we aren't taught that we have Power Over Change and can therefore conquer or subdue change.

---

[8] Senge, Peter *The Fifth Discipline The Art & Practice of The Learning Organization*, New York: Doubleday, 1990, pg. 68

Instead we are taught we have to submit to it and Adapt to Change. Ironically our supposed inferiorities already taught us how to work with changes of all kind.

Likewise we are criticized for our Circular Perspective because it isn't orderly. It is jumbled and confusing as our thoughts seem to just swirl around, not moving forward, going anywhere or producing anything. Men don't understand how our thinking gets us from point A to point Z.

Complexity tells us not to worry about what men think. Their Blue Zone thinking may have been effective in past but today she's rendered it ineffective. She ensures the procedure they are so proud of for taking themselves to point Z, now makes them lost in Timbuktu.

Complexity is telling all of us that the static systematic linear thinking we've always been taught is superior is actually woefully inadequate. When women try to use it to solve complex, technical issues we get often get overwhelmed and frustrated. This leads us to believe that we are incapable of solving these issues and men are better at it. Consequently we turn over work, high-paying roles and entire industries to men. However, after seeing their results we are frustrated again because we see their inadequacies. We think "I could have done it better, if I did it my way." Therein lies our truth.

If women are left alone to think like we want we would realize that our Blue Zone indoctrination has already blended with our Pink Zone characteristics and made us masters at systems thinking. We do it all the time without even knowing it.

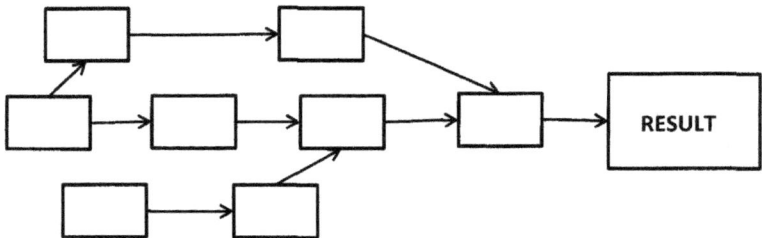

My favorite example of women using systems thinking came from the first woman I ever hired. She was a stay-at-home-mother returning to work. During the interview we wound up discussing her morning routine and how she got everything done. I realized that she was a systems thinker and had skills my all-male staff lacked. After working with her, I appreciated how being stay-at-home-mothers gives women valuable workplace skills that they would otherwise have a hard time developing in a Blue Zone workplace.

Our home is actually one of the best training camps for systems-thinking because there are so many people and activities that need continuous integration. After working in home design and construction, I began seeing the kitchen for the complex system it is and a symbol of women's contribution to the advancement of systems thinking.

Years ago, when men designed homes, the house was fragmented into separate and distinct rooms based on function. I even read a design manual that stated that the kitchen should not be visible from the living room. But today, due to the influence of women, we have open concept designs where the kitchen is the working hub from which we manage the home. We should be very proud of our influence and recognize that we made our homes more systems-driven than most of our workplaces.

To understand how systems thinking works, let's use the example of a mother's morning routine.

In the morning, a mother knows all the activities and how all of the activities must come together to get everyone out of the house on time. She knows what time she has to get up and how far along she should be in getting herself dressed when she wakes up her kids. She knows her daughter must be in the bathroom first and while her daughter is in the shower, she must finish dressing and her son must feed the dog.

Her daughter must be out of the bathroom by the time the weather report comes on the morning news and her husband must immediately slip into the shower. Her son should be going into the bathroom about the same time and she listens for the bathroom door to close. She then goes downstairs to make breakfast and let the dog out. She listens to the morning news and knows that before the sports report is over her son has to be out of the bathroom, the dog let in and breakfast put on the table. Her husband must supervise the kid's breakfast so she can gather up her things.

As she does this, she talks to her husband about his plans for the day so she can plan out the afternoon and evening. When the kids run back upstairs to brush their teeth, she knows she should be grabbing backpacks ensuring homework, snacks and lunches are in each of them. As they head out the door, she knows they are on time if she clicks off the TV as the news anchors are doing their last 5 minutes of happy morning chit-chat.

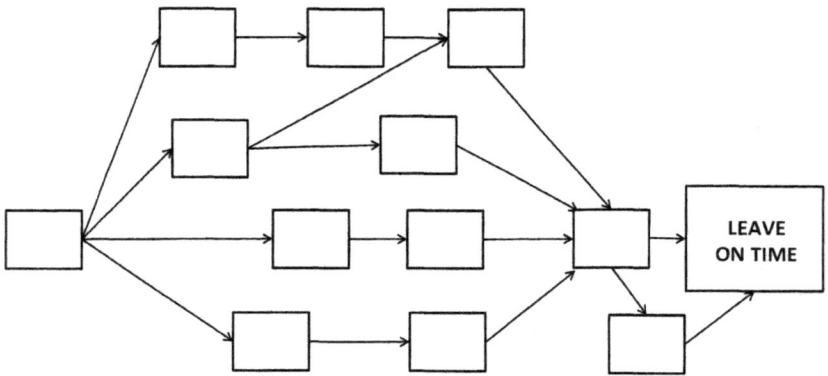

Her morning routine is a complex group of integrated activities. The activities involve getting herself dressed, her daughter dressed, her son dressed, making breakfast, eating breakfast, taking care of the dog and gathering the day's supplies. Together the activities create the daily morning system that gets everyone out of the house on time.

From experience the mother knows that life isn't static and the morning activities can change. Her son plays with the dog instead of getting dressed. Her daughter lingers in the bathroom. Her mother calls. It is raining or snowing. A kid wakes up sick. The car has a flat tire. When any of these happen she immediately thinks about the repercussions and how it affects the rest of the activities.

She thinks holistically and makes the necessary adjustments. Her son who is running late gets handed breakfast bars to eat in the car on the way to school. As she is gathering up backpacks, she also grabs umbrellas for the rain. By continuously thinking and making adjustments to morning system she remains efficient so the desired result of leaving on time still happens.

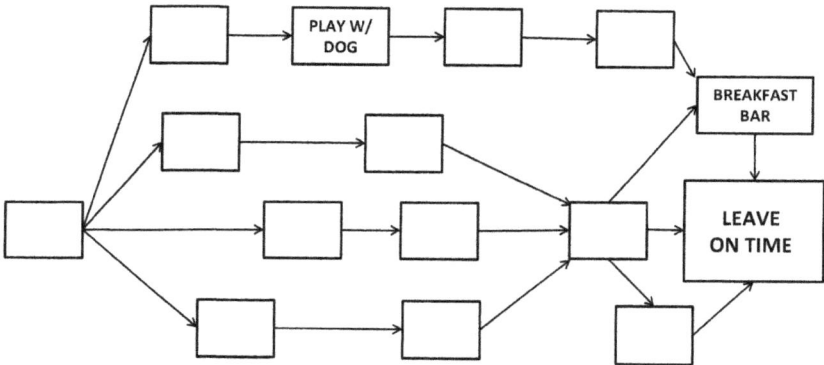

Women's amazing super power to think and work holistically is derived from our characteristics of Group, Circular Perspective, Adapt to Change and our favorite claim to fame, Multiple Task Management. It is further bolstered by our desire to be within and amongst all the activities so we are part of their dynamic interaction. All of this makes us better managers, supervisors and problem-solvers in the workplace.

By being within the system, we are more responsive to changes within it. Our emotional radar gives us great situational awareness. It tells us in real time when the system isn't working like it should. That is why our mother turns on the morning news – it is her timekeeper that allows her to match up TV activities with the morning activities. She can continuously monitor progress and make adjustments without ever looking at a clock or using another device to give her feedback. As women, we want our feedback integrated into our system, not separated or distant from it.

At work we apply these same principles. Our emotional radar tunes us into the daily routine. When we hear something out of the ordinary, we know something is off and we respond. We talk to our colleagues and make adjustments and corrections to the system so we can still get our desired result. If we are supervisors or managers this means we can respond to problems in real time, while they are small and easily corrected.

Meanwhile over in the Blue Zone, our male colleagues stay within the confines of their job descriptions. A supervisor or manager doesn't get down in the weeds because he wants to objectively manage his team from afar. He doesn't see an integrated system, only autonomous individuals with their individual assignments to complete. He relies on dashboards and alerts and alarms on his devices to tell him when something is amiss. He needs the computer system to generate daily, weekly and monthly reports to tell him how well his team functioned. When he tries to go back and figure out what went wrong, Complexity already changed the conditions and his team is focused on a new issue.

They try to draw him in but he doesn't understand working within and amongst his team. He is quickly overwhelmed. He needs them to take Action, so they produce Results, so the computer system can generate a report and he can evaluate the situation. Then he can finally direct them on what to do. But Complexity has already messed with him again and changed conditions. The situation he was addressing is already a lost cause.

I equate this removed method of managing to being a football coach who remains in the locker room while the team is on the field playing. After the game is over and he has all the game statistics, he tells the team what they should have done differently so they can play better next week. As women, we like being the coach who is on the sidelines continuously interacting with the team as they play the game. Our way of continuously interacting within and amongst the team changes the workplace dynamic and we need to take advantage of that by changing how we perceive all the jobs within our workplaces.

Chapter 12
I Can Do that Job!

Most of us are in the Blue Zone because our jobs are in the Blue Zone. Our job descriptions were written by men and for a Blue Zone workplace that is stuck in 19th and 20th century management philosophies. Consequently the job descriptions for traditionally female roles contain artificial limits to restrict women's influence on the Blue Zone workplace. By keeping these jobs small and non-impactful, the lower wages are justified. Likewise the jobs that pay the highest and lead to advancement have descriptions that are written in Blue ink on Blue paper. Men flock to these jobs while women are turned off by them. This is why we must train ourselves to recognize the Blue in our workplaces.

No matter what our job or role is, when we see a lot of Blue in our workplaces, we should also see a lot of Gold. Blue Zone and male-dominated workplaces are a goldmine of opportunity for women, full of Swiss cheese holes crying out for our help. I sought out the deep Blue hard-core male jobs – not to compete with men, or to become a man or to prove that whatever men can do, a woman can do too – but because I knew that was where my greatest opportunities were. I knew that in these deep Blue workplaces, my female characteristics, leveraged correctly, would make a huge and immediate impact. This is how I turned around failing operations and projects in a matter of months and always out-performed my male colleagues.

As women we shouldn't accept our Blue Zone job descriptions as written. Instead we must rewrite our job descriptions using a 21st century perspective where integrating people, tasks, functions, activities, information and parts is critical. When we shift our perspective to integration and to the Purple Zone, we not only expand our traditional roles but we look at the higher paying traditionally male jobs and realize "I can do that job!'

The most extreme example of this that I know of is the job of a construction project superintendent. Construction is considered one of the manliest professions and within construction the project superintendent is considered the most macho job. According to the Blue Zone, it takes a big, strong, loud, intimidating manly-man to stay in there and keeping fighting against the stress, problems and headaches that come from driving a project to completion under time and under budget. However, if we look at the actual job requirements we get a very different understanding of the job.

Construction projects are inherently complex and the project superintendent is responsible for efficiently bringing together all the labor, material and equipment to construct the project. Having done the job, I can tell you it is pure integration. To do the job correctly you have to be out on the construction site within and amongst all the activity so you can hear about problems the moment they arise. Resolving problems quickly requires a lot of personal interaction, on-the-spot collaboration and Purple Zone Teamwork. It also requires recognizing all the repercussions of any change and notifying the impacted team members in the moment. Its high level of integration and holistic thinking makes the job Multiple Task Management nirvana.

Like the entire construction industry, the superintendent's job is in the Purple Zone but way down towards the Pink Zone in the very unmanly shades of lilac, heather and orchid. It is much better suited for women than men. Women like me who went into the job understanding that it is really all about integration, absolutely loved it. Also, a project superintendent doesn't require a college degree even though it is frequently the highest paying job on a construction project. Therefore, we shouldn't be surprised that the Blue Zone continues to promote it as a job for manly-men.

At the opposite end of the manliness spectrum are the engineers. They are far from being macho manly-men but that doesn't stop engineering from being considered an almost pure Blue profession. Blue Zone propaganda tells us that to be good at engineering you have to be good in math and science which also means you have to be logical, rational, analytical and use the type of linear, static thinking women find boring. We are also told that as children, engineers liked taking things apart to see how they worked. This fragmenting is directly opposite to how women enjoy connecting things and immediately tells women that engineering isn't for them. I think the reason I made it through engineering in college was because before I went to college an engineer told me these perceptions weren't true. He told me that engineering is really all about solving complex problems.

In reality engineering is one of the many pure Purple professions. Therefore, at least half of all engineers should be women. When I first began working, I used to joke that engineers made up for the lack of women in the male-dominated workplace. My male colleagues didn't like my joke but there was a lot of truth in it. Engineering, done correctly, requires continuous teamwork, collaboration and integration as it brings a project through the phases of planning, design, procurement, production, commissioning and maintenance.

The Blue Zone screws up engineering because it fragments and separates each of these phases. It systematically "hands off" a project from the planning phase to the design phase. Then, from design to procurement and so on. I spent my entire career fighting against this thinking by introducing integration and holistic project delivery. One of my very first management decisions was to bring production teams into the planning, design and procurement phases. I violated a Blue Zone cardinal rule by forcing the men who worked with their heads to listen to the ideas and opinions of the men who worked with their hands. But by doing so, I brought engineering and project management out of the Blue Zone and into the Purple Zone where it belongs.

Engineering, like so many high paying professions and skilled labor trades, either creates a new system or works on an existing system. They organize work into projects and require project management. Anything "project" should attract women because projects require continuous integration and draw heavily from our Multiple Task Management and Circular Perspective. Many of the old management theories and practices created for manufacturing don't apply to project work. However this doesn't stop Blue Zone workplaces from trying to apply them as they drag project work out of its natural home in the Purple Zone and force it into the Blue Zone. As a project manager I typically saw this reflected in my job descriptions which were a list of duties I could perform autonomously without interacting with most of the project team.

Our Blue Zone workplaces resist and devalue project management because it undermines everything the Blue Zone promotes. Project managers work in a matrix organization which conflicts with the Blue Zone workplace that is organized into functional silos. The Blue Zone likes its functional silos because it allows men to use their Task Expertise to maximize their status and Autonomy. Functional managers consider project managers unwelcome territorial invaders so to protect its functional managers, the Blue Zone workplace limits project manager influence and responsibilities.

On my projects, I asserted myself against functional managers to strengthen my project team and move them back to the Purple Zone where we belonged. To do this I had to continuously point out the inefficiencies, lost time and wasted money created by team members who used their functional silo as an excuse assert their Autonomy. I held the functional managers accountable for these inefficiencies and told them that if they agreed to increase my authority with their team members, I would also assume full accountability. The functional managers jumped at the chance to relinquish their accountability to me. I, however, wanted to make sure that when I successfully delivered the project, I got full credit for its outstanding performance.

Having been a project manager I am never surprised to hear that women are filling the middle management ranks and in excelling that position. We are transforming middle management, and finally, giving a position that has been vague and of questionable value some real meaning. Back in the early days of my career, men used to openly joke that the only thing middle management ever did was create The Great Workplace Mystery: What does a middle manager do all day?

No one ever knew. Of course, middle managers have job descriptions - they generate and read a lot of reports, attend meetings and talk to each other a lot. But what tangible value does any of that add? The question that drifted around male-dominated workplaces: "If your middle manager disappeared would anyone even miss him?"

Sadly the answer to the question was "No." Management was always busy, off doing their thing and the workforce was always busy, off doing theirs. Autonomy and fragmentation ensured there was minimal interaction.

When I walked into the office of my first middle management position, it was obvious that my predecessor had no idea what he was doing and my staff had functioned completely without him. I could tell they were wondering if they could continue to ignore me too.

They quickly learned however, that I was going to be different. I was developing my own ideas of what a middle manager does and I was going to try them out on them. About a year into my job, I read a simple management description that was a better fit to my concept of management:

Workers work in a system.
Managers work on the system with their help.[9]

To me, developing operating systems with my team was so much more interesting than sitting in pointless meetings or on worthless conference calls. Of course, I had my own job duties to do too. But as I looked at my responsibilities I thought that as a manager I should work in a system too so, I created a management system. I then thought my management system and our new computer systems should be fully integrated into my departments' operating systems. It only took me a couple of months to create one large fully integrated system so my teams and I worked together in wholeness. I evolved my management concept, taking it out of the Blue Zone where management and workers are distinct and separate and into the Purple Zone where we are fully integrated:

Managers and Workers work in a system.
Together, Managers and Workers work on the system to improve it.

My management concept goes back to the idea of being the coach who is on sidelines during the game continuously interacting with the team while they play so they get their best performance. I also learned that once I created the whole system, many of my management responsibilities became automatic and others were super-fast and easy to complete. This gave me a lot more time to work with my teams and our customers to prevent problems and continuously improve our performance.

The idea that managers are part of the system helps women feel comfortable moving up into senior management positions because it allows us to keep our Circular Perspective. We don't have to adopt the Blue Zone Linear Perspective that says we have to disconnect

---

[9] Tribus, Myron "Managing To Survive In A Competitive World", *Quality First Selected Papers on Quality and Productivity Improvement*, National Society of Profession Engineers Publication #1459, 1988, pg. 32

from the rest of the organization and be up on the top of the organizational hierarchy all by ourselves. As women we should view moving up to mean that we have more people, equipment, functions, information and systems to integrate up, down and all around the organization. It means we are in the middle of (not on top of) a much larger system.

In senior management our responsibilities typically focus our attention on profit and loss. Our Blue Zone management training tells us we don't have the time to work on systems, integration or be within and amongst the people in our organization. However, as a middle manager and project manager I discovered something amazing about working in a holistic system - I always knew where we stood financially. By being part of the system, I could read the system just as if I were reading real time financial reports. Running the monthly financial reports became a formality because I already knew within a few thousand dollars our financial position on projects worth tens of millions of dollars.

By the time I was a senior manager I knew our management and operating systems inside and out, backwards and forwards. I knew how to configure and format financial reports so reading them was just like reading a detailed report on the performance of our operating systems. I could look at numbers and identify specific operational problems. Even as a senior manager I continued to focus on the systems and how my teams functioned to improve our margins. I liked to say "If you take care of the systems integration, the dollars will take care of themselves."

Throughout my career I never felt I had to do my job the way my peers or predecessors did it. This freed me from Blue Zone job descriptions so my teams and I could explore new ways of working and managing. It never mattered how high or how low I was in the workplace hierarchy, I always seized my empowerment to develop a better Purple Zone approach to my jobs. This is how I always out-performed my colleagues. I could then leverage my performance with the meritocracy to advance myself.

The best part of working in the Purple Zone is that I could be me — even in hard core male jobs. I discovered the many shades of Purple that fit my personality and I learned how to use them in various workplace situations to the benefit of my workplace and colleagues. This is where real self-confidence and personal fulfillment come from.

Chapter 13
Women's Purple Zone
Leadership

When I began my website in 2012, I created the tagline:

Empowering Women to Lead the Male-Dominated Workplace

It expresses how only women can lead men and the male-dominated workplace to the Purple Zone. Many women however have trepidation about leading men because we only know the Blue Zone definition of leadership. Most of us don't know that we don't have to lead this way because we have our own incredible leadership style that allows us to lead our way.

When we think of leadership, we typically picture a leader who is out in front of his followers. He is the leader because he was confident enough to step forward, put himself out there in front of the group and convince everyone that he knows what to do. Leadership is a vulnerable position because people often challenge you. They disagree with you and tell you that you are wrong. Some people want to replace you as the leader in order to advance their point of view or themselves.

Since being a leader can be difficult, it's easy to understand why many women don't want to be leaders and especially don't want to be leaders to a group of men. That is why we shouldn't use this Blue

Zone definition of leadership. Instead we move leadership to the Purple Zone where we are encouraged to step up and lead our way.

As a project manager I was the project leader, in charge of a matrix organization where I had limited authority over many of my team members. I had to lead through cooperation. So, I called upon my Circular perspective to see myself as the hub of a wheel, coordinating the activities and processes of the project's various functions, departments and personnel who were connected to me through the spokes.

Unlike our typical perception of a leader, I wasn't out in front of everyone and I didn't use a Blue Zone hierarchy to give myself status to exercise my authority over others. Instead I stood amongst my team and my leadership gave me power with my team. I was empowered as was every member of my team.

In project management, senior management and complex environments, a leader oversees many tasks or functions. The leader isn't an expert in each one and can't determine the solution to every problem or the answer to every question on their own. The leader must rely on the input of others. When the leader is on top of a hierarchy, the Linear Perspective restricts interaction and information is filtered as it makes its way to the leader. This style of leadership can't produce the best solution.

However, when we use our Circular perspective to stand amongst people interaction is not limited. We can talk to everyone and draw on the collective expertise of the entire Purple Zone team. Leadership with people produces collaboration, synergy, integration and coordination – the behaviors that women excel at but also produce the best solutions.

For women to become comfortable as leaders, we begin by exercising our personal leadership as good team members.

We must recognize that we are assigned to a team because we have skills and expertise the team needs. As a team member we are responsible for stepping forward with our skills each time we recognize the team needs them. We don't compete against fellow team members to assert our opinions and ideas over top of theirs so we can declare ourselves the winner or MVP. Instead, we look for what our team is missing and for the Swiss cheese holes that require our experience and skills.

To be a good team member we can't sit back and wait to be called upon before we speak up or assert ourselves because our team leader and other team members may not know our skills are needed. Therefore, we must be amongst our team so we are aware of what our fellow team members are doing. Whenever a fellow team member takes action that impacts us, we are responsible for stepping forward and letting the team know how we are impacted. To have a fully functioning Purple Zone team, each team member must exercise their personal leadership.

As good team members we also exercise our personal leadership in support of the greater common good. When our workplace takes actions that adversely affects team morale or performance we need to make a leadership decision. We can look at our position in the organizational hierarchy and believe we aren't in the right position or high enough to speak up or do anything. Or, we can see ourselves as a Purple Zone team member who has a responsibility to speak up.

Of course, someone with a hierarchal perspective can always challenge us or dismiss us, but that shouldn't be the reason we don't speak up. In my experience it often comes back to bite them and I get an "I told you so" moment. I find that I am listened to a little bit more the next time. So, even though there was a delay, my personal leadership resulted in a small but positive step forward. This after all is what leadership really does. It begins the slow, progressive journey of moving in a new and better direction.

The Blue Zone often uses management and leadership interchangeably but they are very different. I think of management as a position in the organizational hierarchy that works within the status quo. Leadership however, is about creating change and can be exercised by anyone in the organization. While non-leaders accept things the way they are even if they don't like them, leaders improve, change or disrupt the status quo. To be a leader you must believe in your point of view and that you have the inherent right to express it. You have to be willing to step into the arena and assert yourself. That can be scary, especially when you are in the arena by yourself and the only voice with that point of view. However, that is how great changes begin.

"A good leader leads the people from above them. A great leader leads the people from within them." – M.D. Arnold

"The task of the leader is to get their people from where they are to where they have not been." – Henry Kissinger

"The function of leadership is to produce more leaders, not more followers." – Ralph Nader

Chapter 14
Empowered Women Shine
in the Arena

My website tagline uses another important word – Empowering. Contrary to the popular definition of empowerment, I don't believe anyone else can empower you. I believe that you are inherently empowered and it is your choice as to how much you step into and assert your empowerment.

Men have always been told they must step into their empowerment because the workplace judges them on how much they get involved, take action and make things happen. My mentors explained this to me very early in my career and I decided that if I wanted to advance as far as I could in my career, then I had to assume my empowerment and be someone who could always be depended upon to step forward and make things happen. This decision is what made me the woman in the room.

Throughout my career I watched the male-dominated workplace sort through and weed out men who wouldn't or couldn't act. They were sent off to staff jobs, consulting firms or government jobs to shuffle paper. This sorting created a divide in the male-dominated workplace between the Doers who acted and the Intellectuals who couldn't.

As time went on and Complexity became more powerful and influential, the Intellectuals began asserting themselves. Their papers, studies and plans found their way back into action-oriented workplaces. When the Doers were handed the work of Intellectuals, they immediately filed it in the trash can. The Doers, in spite of all their Blue Zone indoctrination and manly personas, suddenly went Pink believing you actually had to be in and amongst the work in order to understand how things really get done. Listening to their reaction, I discovered that the best Doers often worked close to the Purple Zone and even temporarily crossed into it when there was a real crisis and failure was not an option. These outwardly gruff men were the easiest for me to lead to the Purple Zone because they unknowingly already understood it. The Intellectuals however, remained deeply vested in their Blue Zone thinking, using it to challenge the superior workplace status of the Doers.

All through my career I monitored the divide between the Intellectuals and the Doers. In 1991, I wrote my first article "The Great American Alligator Slayer" [10] about the power and status of Doers who represented the male-dominated workplace's ideal man. Over the years, I watched the divide widened and new factions of men form. Each new faction challenged the others for their right to claim that they represented the Blue Zone's ideal, superior man. As I wasted countless hours in conference rooms watching their fights play out, I amused myself by writing my own satirical story of these battles for status which I called "Swamp Wars."[11]

I first knew that the male-dominated workplace had changed dramatically and become consumed by "Swamp Wars" when the protégé of a former Intellectual colleague showed up on a construction site. He was an Intellectual whose sole purpose was to

---

[10] Callihan, Dorothy. "The Great American Alligator Slayer." The Woman In The Room. 29 May 2012, http://thewomanintheroom.com/2012/05/29/the-great-american-alligator-slayer/

[11] Callihan, Dorothy. "Swamp Wars – This Century's Battle for Status." The Woman In The Room. 7 April 2012 http://thewomanintheroom.com/2012/09/07/swamp-wars-this-centurys-battle-for-status/

critique our performance. Obviously, this didn't go over well with my colleagues who were action-oriented Alligator Slayers and we wasted a phenomenal amount of time and money fighting Swamp Wars.

On my next project, there was no shortage of Intellectuals (and Intellectual-Wannabes) who thought their sole purpose in life was to critique how well the Doers did their job. An ugly Swamp War broke out that waged on for months, again wasting valuable time and money. One day one of my frustrated team members brought me this quote from Teddy Roosevelt:

> "It is not the critic who counts; not the man who points out how the strong man stumbles, or where the doer of deeds could have done them better. The credit belongs to the man who is actually in the arena, whose face is marred by dust and sweat and blood; who strives valiantly; who errs, who comes short again and again, because there is no effort without error and shortcoming; but who does actually strive to do the deeds; who knows great enthusiasms, the great devotions; who spends himself in a worthy cause; who at the best knows in the end the triumph of high achievement, and who at the worst, if he fails, at least fails while daring greatly, so that his place shall never be with those cold and timid souls who neither know victory nor defeat."[12]

I made many copies of this quote and hung them all over the construction office walls and doors. I took particular satisfaction in taping one copy on the conference room wall directly across from where the lead Intellectual-critic sat.

In the end, our Intellectual-critics were dismissed because just as my mentors told me years earlier, it is always the people in the arena - the Doers and the Achievers - that our workplaces ultimately rely

---

[12] The Man In The Arena, Excerpt from the speech "Citizenship In A Republic" delivered at the Sorbonne, in Paris, France on 23 April, 1910

on for their continued existence. There is no product, service or profit without Doers and Achievers. This is a fundamental truth to all businesses that women must understand and heed if we are to advance in the workplace and close the wage gap.

Historically, women weren't allowed or expected to get in the arena. We were expected to sit in the stands as adoring fans or stand along the sidelines as cheerleaders while men played in the arena, accomplishing the great deeds. The women's liberation and feminist movements fought to give women the opportunity to go into the arena, if we want.

Today, we still have the option to play it safe by remaining in the stands or along the sidelines. This is where many of our male colleagues expect us to be or believe we really want to be.

Complexity however, is screaming a new message to us. She is telling us we can no longer sit up in the stands or be cheerleaders on the sidelines. We must lift up our half of the sky, take it into the arena and assume our rightful place alongside men as Doers of great deeds. It is the only way to end Swamp Wars and the fragmentation, division and polarization that goes along with it. It is the only way to move past egotistical fighting for status so the greater common good can be achieved.

For many women going into the arena is a frightening and terrifying thought. So we have to question, what it is that we are really are afraid of? As I thought about that question, this quote by from Marianne Williamson kept coming into my life:

"Our deepest fear is not that we are inadequate. Our deepest fear is that we are powerful beyond measure. It is our light, not our darkness that frightens us. We ask ourselves "Who am I to be brilliant, gorgeous, talented, fabulous?" Actually who are you not to be? You are a child of God. Your playing small doesn't serve the world. There is nothing enlightened about shrinking so that other people won't feel insecure around you. We were born to manifest the glory of God that is within us. It's not just in some of us; it's in everyone. And as we let our own light shine, we unconsciously give other people permission to do the same. As we are liberated from our own fear, our presence automatically liberates others."[13]

Isn't it odd that we would be afraid of our own power? But if you think about it, that is exactly what we are really afraid of and the real reason women aren't advancing.

If we believe we are powerful, then we feel responsible to step forward and serve the world. But then when we put ourselves out there, we open ourselves up to ridicule, critique, questioning and possibly failure. There is the possibility that the power we felt within ourselves can be taken away. So in order to protect our power, we hide it - we play it safe by playing small.

We are further encouraged to play it small and see ourselves as disempowered so we don't diminish and disempower others. We are taught to see the world through men's Linear Perspective which tells us that for one person to rise up, another person must be torn down because there is a fixed amount of superior places and a fixed quantity of power.

As women we shouldn't believe there is a fixed quantity of power and for one person to rise up another must be diminished. We shouldn't believe that to be powerful and brilliant we have to compare ourselves to others and be judged as better than them. Instead we know these qualities originate from within ourselves and we project them outward as an expression of who we are. So when we express our power we are saying "This is how I shine." And it makes us look around to others and say "Tell me how you shine too."

To exercise our female power, we must look to our female Energy Projection and Circular Perspective. When we see people in a circle, we recognize each person as an equal, unique individual and value them for who they are. Each person is a vital part of the whole. We

---

[13] Williamson, Marianne *A Return to Love: Reflections on the Principles of A Course in Miracles,* New York: HarperCollins Publishers, 1992

can each say "This is who I am" without diminishing other people – we only add ourselves to the sum of the whole.

I think of our Circle Perspective as a container. Each person adds to the whole and each person's contribution of themselves only increases how much the circle contains. So as we express ourselves and project our energy, it isn't dissipated or consumed. It is captured. It interacts with and influences the energy of others. This is how we get to experience our own inherent power. But more importantly is how the Purple Zone becomes a greenhouse that cultivates the positive energy to serve the greater common good.

Contrast our female perspective to how the Blue Zone taught us to think about our personal power. The Linear male Perspective doesn't create a mechanism to collect and contain everyone's power.

So then, why aren't we taught to think through a circular perspective?

Because it doesn't produce the individual heroes the Blue Zone promises us. We have subordinated the collective energy of many in order to pursue the dream of the ideal individual who is as powerful as the collective many. When we hold ourselves back and play it safe we are hoping there is superhero out there who is stronger, more powerful and better in every way than us to justify us playing it safe. But there isn't. There are only lots and lots of other ordinary people just like us.

We have a choice in our perspective. We can choose to play it small and wait for the elusive ultimate hero or we can step forward, lift up our half of the sky and let our shining powerful selves encourage others to join us. In writing these books, I am embracing my female perspective and inviting other women to join me in allowing themselves to shine in hope of creating a great big beautiful circle with boundless amounts of both male and female energy. My hope for the 21st century is that women embrace their inherent feminine power and take it into the arena because that is what the world desperately needs.

As a final thought, let me give you a glimpse into the new reality the Purple Zone creates when we blend the two quotes – one of which tends to be Blue and the other Pink:

Our deepest fear is not that we are inadequate. Our deepest fear is that we are powerful beyond measure; that we have the power to step into the arena and strive valiantly. We don't fear dust and sweat and blood, we don't fear coming up short again and again. We fear being brilliant, gorgeous, talented and fabulous.

So, we listen to the critic who doesn't count; to the person who points out how we stumble or how we as the doer of deeds could have done better.

Then we realize our playing small doesn't serve the world. There is nothing enlightening about shrinking so that the critics won't feel insecure around us. We know we were born to manifest the glory of God that is within us. We know it's not just in some of us, it's in everyone and when we let our own light shine, we unconsciously give other people permission to do the same.

So, we go back into the arena. We may err. We may come up short. But we will strive to do the deeds, to know great enthusiasms and great devotions. We will spend ourselves in a worthy cause knowing at best we will end in the triumph of high achievement. But if we fail, at least we fail while daring greatly. We know we liberated ourselves from our own fear and our presence automatically liberated others so they are never with those cold and timid souls who neither know victory nor defeat.

Chapter 15
Move Forward with a
New Perspective

My goal for this book is to challenge and expand your perceptions about your workplace, your value within it and the opportunities it presents to you. I hope that you experienced a few mind shifts of your own or said to yourself, "Hmm, I never thought about it that way."

I deliberately didn't go into a detailed description about each of the male and female balancing characteristics because I first want you to pause and take a fresh look at your own society and workplace. I want you to become aware of how they favor male energy and how they implement male characteristics as the superior standard. I want you to think about how old narratives, the Doctrine of Two Spheres, stereotypes and your own Blue Zone indoctrination all contribute to your perceptions. Take a moment to broaden your own perspective about how your workplace really functions.

Look for Autonomy - I guarantee you will see a lot more of it than you thought. Observe how your workplaces fragments people, activities and information and what your workplace does to maintain this fragmentation. Pay attention to management and how much they interact with the workforce and coordinate its daily activities. Become aware of how much work that was supposed to get done, didn't get done because things didn't come together the way they should. Acknowledge which workplace procedures and computer systems don't work the way you need them to.

Use your emotional radar to pick up on what doesn't seem right. Tune into what you are feeling and your own instincts – give yourself permission to believe that what you are feeling is actually right. Start noting what frustrates you and when you think the guys are taking shortcuts, missing things or just don't get it. Make a mental note of your "I told you so" moments - all the times you are dismissed and the guys did it their way only to prove you were right all along.

Catch yourself in those moments when you choose not to assert yourself. Think about why you don't and what is holding you back. Is your Blue Zone indoctrination coming through? Are you being intimidated by Blue Zone propaganda? Or are you just afraid to shine because you believe it diminishes others, especially your male colleagues?

By becoming situationally-aware of both yourself and your workplace, you start seeing what is missing and what doesn't work. You start seeing the Swiss cheese holes and realizing they are opportunities for you to assert yourself and lift up your half of the sky. You start seeing all the ways in which your workplace needs you and the value you bring.

In my next book I will go into detail about the male and female balancing characteristics and how we use them to create the Purple Zone. In future books I also will discuss the Blue Zone male-dominated workplace and how to be a successful woman working in the Purple Zone. I realize that many women will want my last book first because they just want to know the "10 Most Important Things Every Woman Should Do To Be Successful." However, checklist solutions like this are pure Blue Zone thinking and will only serve to draw you into the Blue Zone. So, I won't go there.

The reality is that there are no shortcuts or checklist solutions to workplace success or personal fulfillment. There is only choosing to go into the arena and thinking your way through the situations and problems you encounter. That is why we need to hear from more women who can say, "Been there, dealt with that, let me tell you what worked." We need more women to join me in sharing their knowledge and experience about how we hold up our half of the sky. While we are only beginning to discover the unique value women bring to the workplace there is one thing for certain – our workplaces need us.

About the Author

Dorothy (Dot) Callihan is a civil engineer with over 30 years of experience in facilities management and construction. She began her career as an Air Force officer where she worked in Civil Engineering Operations. In the Air Force she discovered her passions for leadership and working with the craftsmen who turn the wrenches and operate the heavy equipment. After separating from the Air Force she continued working in facilities management as a consultant revolutionizing the industry. As an Air Force spouse she and her family continued to move around the country and Dot transitioned into home-building through her service in Volunteers In Service to America (VISTA) with Habitat for Humanity. Inspired by her history of service, she remained committed to doing construction that has meaning and purpose. Her experience and passions came together when she entered the military family housing construction industry. For 12 years, she traveled around the country finally tearing down and reconstructing the military family housing communities that were substandard when she was an Air Force officer 20 years earlier. As that industry wound down, she set her sights on her longtime goal of mixing construction and adventure. She achieved her goal by becoming the General Manager of a construction company working in the Canadian oil sands. However, a new mission was calling her.

Dot was often the first female peer and manager her male colleagues worked with and as such experienced the pure male-dominated workplace. Recognizing its shortcomings she was determined to fix how the male-dominated workplace functions in order to end the high levels of stress, chaos and crises that were common in her workplaces. Her original goal was to write a business book primarily for men but that idea changed when she figured out that being a woman was the critical factor in transforming her workplaces and improving performance. Her focus changed to using her experience to help women assert and advance themselves in the workplace so they can create the workplace we all want.

In 2012 Dot launched her website The Woman In The Room to share her experiences and knowledge as a woman who pursued a non-traditional career. Today, she remains committed to her original goal of improving the male-dominated workplace but now she does it by "Empowering Women to Lead the Male-Dominated Workplace."

Dot received her Bachelor's Degree in Civil Engineering from Virginia Tech and her Master's Degree in Engineering Management from the University of Alaska, Fairbanks

www.ingramcontent.com/pod-product-compliance
Lightning Source LLC
Chambersburg PA
CBHW071600040426
42452CB00008B/1241